GOD'S WILL BE DONE

TRADITIONAL PSYCHOETHICS
AND PERSONALITY PARADIGM

Laleh Bakhtiar

Library of Congress Cataloging in Publication Data

Bakhtiar, Laleh
   God's Will Be Done

   Includes bibliographical references.
   1. Psychology, Religious. 2. Consciousness.
3. Ethics. I. Bakhtiar, Laleh. II. Title.
BL53.U45   200'.19   75.16302
ISBN: 1-56744-429-6 (pbk)

Published by:
The Institute of Traditional Psychoethics and Guidance

Distributed by:
KAZI Publications, Inc.
3023-27 West Belmont Avenue
Chicago, IL 60618
(312) 267-7001

CONTENTS

"...be not like those
who forgot God and
[eventually]
God caused them
to forget their 'self'...."
(59:18-19)

THE GREATER JIHAD CIRCLE OF SELF-RENEWAL*

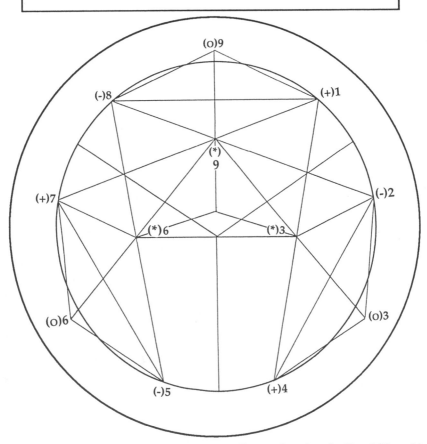

*Just as numbers and geometry are significant in Creation based on the Sign, " *We send it not down but in known measure*" (15:21), they also form the basis for the renewal of the self in the completion of the perfection of nature in its mode of operation within the self. For the methods provided by psychoethics to effect change, see *Jihad Phase I: Traditional Guidance and Centering the Self.*

THE GREATER JIHAD
CIRCLE OF SELF-RENEWAL (CONT'D)

0		Divine Essence is symbolized by zero in the sense that it is above knowing.
1	•	The point (one) generates the **Circle of Self-renewal of the Greater Jihad,** symbolizing one, unity, the principle and origin of all numbers. The point also symbolizes the self centered in Justice when the self has: *Received Divine Assistance *Attained Balance in Wisdom, Courage and Temperance *Benefitted Another Human Being Because of Self-balance.
2	——	The point moves and generates the line that then forms the segment .

THE GREATER JIHAD
CIRCLE OF SELF-RENEWAL (CONT'D)

3

DIVINE
SPIRIT

PRE-
SERVE
SPECIES

PRE-
SERVE
INDI-
VIDUAL

1

INTELLECT

ATTRAC-
TION TO
PLEASURE

AVOID-
ANCE OF
HARM/PAIN

2

COGNITION

AFFECT/
EMOTIVE

BEHAV-
IOR

3

BRAIN

LIVER
(GUT)

HEART

4

CAPABLE OF
CONSCIOUSNESS

UNCON-
SCIOUS-
NESS

PRECON-
SCIOUS-
NESS

5

The three-fold division of the circle divides the self into three basic parts which operate at six different levels:

*Level 1: Spiritual/Biological

*Level 2: Psychological (1)

*Level 3: Psychological (2)

*Level 4: Physiological: Source of Energy

*Level 5: Cognitive

THE GREATER JIHAD
CIRCLE OF SELF-RENEWAL (CONT'D)

3

*Level 6: Psychoethics

4

The center of Level 6 marks the center of a triangle symbolizing justice, the positive trait that develops when the self is balanced in the other three traits.

This, then, forms a triangle within the three-fold division where justice falls in the center. These four positive traits symbolize the psychoethics given to the self by nature in its mode of operation.

Their being balanced is symbolized by (*). Centeredness takes place when the positive trait, symbolzing movement towards center, of each of the three segments is at its respective center

THE GREATER JIHAD
CIRCLE OF SELF-RENEWAL (CONT'D)

7

(o)9

(-)8   (+)1

(*)9

(-)7   (-)2

(*)6 (*)3

(o)6   (o)3

(-)5   (+)4

The movement of change, growth, and restoration to health is indicated by the number 7 as the symbol of movement in the universe and renewal within the self. The self, as has been shown, consists of three basic pspychological systems: cognitive, behavior, and affect. The self psychoethically has four basic positive traits: Wisdom, Courage, Temperance, and Justice. When unity (1) is divided by 7, a recurring decimal is obtained which is indicated on the Greater Jihad symbol by the moving line: 1, 4, 2, 8, 5, 7 and back to 1. There are no 3s, 6s, or 9s. The same numbers are obtained with 1/7 +1/7 and so forth six times. The numbers are the same, but fall in a different order. Although there are no 3s, 6s, or 9s, the movement of change line passes through the positive traits at the edges of the triangle located in the center, namely (*9), (*6), and (*3).

THE GREATER JIHAD
CIRCLE OF SELF-RENEWAL (CONT'D)

9

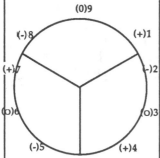

(0)9
(-)8
(+)1
(+)7
(-)2
(0)6
(0)3
(-)5
(+)4

Cognitive System:
Positive trait is
Wisdom (*9):
-8: Preconsciousness (knowing that you do not know)
+1: Overconsciousness (knowing but deceiving the self)
o9: Unconsciousnessness (not knowing and not knowing that you do not know)

Behavioral System:
Positive Trait is
Courage (*3):
-2: Cowardice
+4: Excessive anger
o3: Fear of Other than God

Affective System:
Positive Trait is
Temperance (*6):
-5 Apathy
+7 Excessive lust
o6 Grief/Envy

Through the nurturing process, each of the three positive traits of nature may develop an imbalance. This imbalance is of two types: an imbalance in quantity of the positive trait or in the quality. An imbalance in quantity develops into two conditions and an imbalance in quality, in terms of the positive trait, develops into one condition. They are:

Imbalance in Quantity:
(+) Overdevelopment or
(-) Underdevelopment
Imbalance in Quality:
(o) Undevelopment

These appear on the circumference of the circle, the farthest distance from the positive trait near the center.

Although negative traits that develop are innumerable, the most chronic are described in psychoethics as examples.

It is to be noted that all three imbalances are negative traits because they are in excess of moderation, off the Straight Path. o9, o6, and o3 indicate an imbalance in terms of quality of the positive trait and, therefore, fall outside the circle of self-renewal.

THE GREATER JIHAD
CIRCLE OF SELF-RENEWAL (CONT'D)

3
6
9

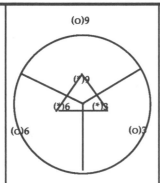

3, 6, and 9 are numbers which do not appear in the movement of change line, yet they play a significant role in self-renewal. They symbolize the depravity of a positive trait symbolized by (o) when they fall outside the circle of self-renewal as well as the positive trait itself (*). They are significant numbers to unity because they also produce recurring decimals. 1 divided by 3 = .333 or 1/3. 1/3 + 1/3 = 2/3 = .666. .666 + .333 = .999. When the final third is added, the result is endless nines. Recurring nines becomes the symbol of unity of the self which, no matter to what extent it perfects nature in its mode of operation, it is still imperfect in relation to the Creator. 3, 6, and 9 symbolizes the highest traits of balance and centeredness (*) as well as depravity of the positive trait in terms of quality (o). As negative traits (o), they fall outside the circle of self as undevelopment of the positive trait.

THE GREATER JIHAD
CIRCLE OF SELF-RENEWAL (CONT'D)

1
2
3
4
5
6
7
8
9

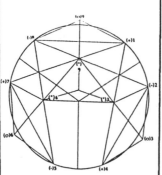

The Circle of Self-renewal shows both the nature/nurture aspects of self. The self is either centered in the positive traits, having completed Phase I of the Greater Jihad and ready to begin Phase II or uncentered and out of sync in which case methods of restoration to the healthy self are needed (see *Jihad Phase I: Centering the Self*).

PREFACE

This personality paradigm is essentially that of monotheism and unity, the world view that "there is no god, but God" or "there is no deity, but God." It is to see the universe and all that is in it as aspects of the One God. The world view of monotheism (*tawhid*) forms the underlying basis for psychoethics, in general, and its personality paradigm, in particular. The monotheist (*Hanif*) regards the whole universe as a unity, as a single form, a single living and conscious thing, possessing will, intelligence, feeling, and purpose, revolving in a just and orderly system in which there is no discrimination no matter what one's gender, color, race, class, or faith be. All comes from God and returns to God, while a multitheist (*mushrik*) views the universe as a discordant assemblage full of disunity, contradiction, and heterogeneity containing many independent and conflicting poles, unconnected desires, customs, purposes, wills, sexes, sects, colors, races, classes, and faiths.

The monotheistic world view sees the universal unity in existence, a unity of three separate relationships: the self and God, the self and nature, including other human beings, and the self and self. These relationships are not alien to one another; there are no boundaries between them. They move in the same direction. Other religious world views see the Divinity or even the plural of this as existing in a special, metaphysical world of the gods, a higher world as contrasted with the lower world of nature and matter. They teach that God is separate from the world, created it and then left it alone. In the monotheistic world view, God has never left and is the goal of the return of the self. Here the self fears only one Power and is answerable to only one Judge; turns to one direction (*qiblah*), directing all hopes and desires to only one Source. A belief in monotheism gives the self a sense of independence and liberation from everything other than God and a connectedness to the universe and all that it contains. Submission to God's Will alone liberates the self from worshipping anything other than God and rebelling against anything that purports to be God.

*****

There are so many people to thank for their generous support over the years that a separate volume could be written in order to mention all of them. However, I will be concise and, first of all, thank my family: Jamshid, Cyrus, my beloved deceased brother, Lailee, Shireen, Parveen, Paree, Maryam, Parvaneh, and Afsoneh Bakhtiar; my children: Karim, Davar, and Mani Ardalan. Next I would like to thank my teachers: Javad Nurbakhsh, Seyyid Hossein Nasr, Jamshid Bakhtiar, William Chittick, Sachiko Murata, Sayyid Gulzar Haider, Nader Ardalan, and Andrew Burgess. Also, I thank Kazi Publications, Inc for believing in this work and encouraging me to complete it and Jamshid Bakhtiar, Riazuddin Riaz, Seyyid Gulzar Haider, and Christopher Fitzpatrick for their invaluable comments on the manuscript. May God's Will Be Done.

Laleh Bakhtiar
Chicago, December, 1992

1

OVERVIEW

INTRODUCTION

There is a famous story about a contest that was held between Greek and Chinese artists as to which group had the better artists. Each was given a room which faced each other, separated by a door so that they could not see each other's work. The Greeks decorated the walls with beautiful flowers using rare colors and techniques. The Chinese, on the other hand, polished the surface of the walls in their room. When the door between them was removed, the beautiful art of the Greeks was reflected on the wall of the Chinese in all of its original beauty and splendor. The Chinese won the contest because their creative solution most clearly represented the role of the human self in creation. [1]

In the traditional perspective, nature, aspects of which were re-created by the Greeks, and the self as mirror, re-created by the Chinese, are both reflections of the One God's self-disclosure in the Divine Name "Creator." The connection between nature and the self is seen to be not in matter or physical form, but in the creative process itself. This creative process is known as "nature in its mode of operation."

Nature in its mode of operation is the means by which the Divine Presence in creation continues. Creation is not considered to have been a one time "big bang" from which God then retired from the universe, but an ongoing process of re-creation. With every expansion-contraction, with every breathing out and breathing in, all of nature, including the human self, dies and is reborn through the Creative Act. This death and rebirth occurs through Divine Guidance, the second most important Divine Name for traditional psychology being *al-Hadi*, the Guide.

This Divine Guidance which guides nature in its mode of operation has established a means of communications between the Creator and the self which consists of Signs. *We* (God the Creator) *shall show them* (human beings) *Our Signs upon the horizon* (universe) *and within themselves* (the self) *until it is clear to them* (human beings) *that He* (God) *is the Real* (*haqq*)." (41:53) When the human being becomes conscious of self and then freely chooses to learn to read and to live by the Signs without and within, God's Will is done. Such a person will have completed the perfection of nature in its mode of operation within the self, will be centered, having gained experiential knowledge of the oneness of God (monotheism, *tawhid*) reflected in nature and within themselves.

TRADITIONAL PSYCHOLOGY

Signs of God in nature, which includes all of the universe from the largest galaxy of stars and the planets to the smallest living organism on earth, are both external to the human being and internal. Knowledge of external signs

FIRST CLASSIFICATION OF THE SCIENCES

PHILOSOPHICAL SCIENCES
(SAME IN ALL PERIODS)

THEORETICAL

METAPHYSICS
(SUPREME SCIENCE)

MATHEMATICS
(INTERMEDIATE SCIENCE)

NATURAL PHILOSOPHY
(LOWER SCIENCES)

PERTAINING TO THE INDIVIDUAL
(ETHICS)

PRACTICAL

PERTAINING TO THE COLLECTIVE
(ECONOMICS/POLITICS)

NON-RELIGIOUS

NON-PHILOSOPHICAL SCIENCES
(NOT SAME IN ALL PERIODS)

RELIGIOUS

INTELLECTUAL

TRANSMITTED

SECOND CLASSIFICATION OF THE SCIENCES

EARLY (AWA'IL)

PRACTICAL PHILOSOPHY INCLUDING ETHICS, POLITICS, ECONOMICS

THEORETICAL PHILOSOPHY INCLUDING LOGIC, PRIME PHILOSOPHY, METAPHYSICS,
SCIENCE OF NATURAL BODIES AND ALL BRANCHES OF NATURAL PHILOSOPHY

PRINCIPLES OF MATHEMATICS INCLUDING ARITHMETIC, GEOMETRY, ASTRONOMY,
AND MUSIC

BRANCHES OF NATURAL PHILOSOPHY INCLUDING MEDICINE, ALCHEMY, NATURAL
MAGIX, ETC.

BRANCHES OF MATHEMATICS INCLUDING ALL BRANCHES OF ASTRONOMY, MATHE-
MATICAL GEOGRAPHY, MECHANICAL DEVICES, CHESS, AND BACKGAMMON

LATE (AWAKHIR)

LITERATURE, SCIENCES OF THE DIVINE LAW, SUFISM, SCIENCES OF DAILY DIS-
COURSE SUCH AS HISTORY, BIOGRAPHY, GENEALOGY, ETC.

1: Classification of the Sciences according to Amuli (15th century). From Seyyid Hossein Nasr, *Islamic Science: an Illustrated Study.*

forms the subject of the various natural sciences the human being has developed to "understand" the Divine Creation like cosmology, astronomy, philosophy, biology, chemistry, and so forth as well as the science of revelation, gaining knowledge about the Quran where the 6000 some verses are each called a Sign (*ayah*) (fig. 1).

Understanding of Signs within develops through the Natural Sciences—the branch known as Medicine—and Philosophy—and the branch known as Practical Philosophy. From the 13th century to the present in the Muslim world, the latter science has included three branches: the Science of Ethics, the Science of Economics (including Home Economics) and the Science of Politics. Traditional psychology is found in the Science of Ethics and can, therefore, most clearly be referred to as psychoethics.

In order to develop a fair evaluation of psychoethics, in general, and its personality paradigm, in particular, it is necessary to understand its perspective on the human being's place in the universe, a perspective which is both holistic and integrative.

THE COVENANT BETWEEN SELF AND GOD

As the last creation of nature's Creator, the human being occupies a special place in nature because out of all of nature God breathes His Spirit within the human self alone. It is this infusion of the Divine Spirit which allows the human self to become conscious of self, an advantage no other aspect of nature has. Therefore, even though all of nature, the universe, and the cosmos are divinely created from the combination of natural elements and their qualities, only the human form has "consciousness of self."

In the traditional perspective this gift of consciousness was granted to the potential human spirit when it accepted the trust of the heavens and the earth. *"We offered the trust to the heavens and the earth and the mountains, but they refused to carry it and were afraid of it, and the human being carried it."* (33:72) The acceptance of the trust includes the covenant with the Lord (Rabb) as the Quran says, *"And when your Lord took the seed of the children of Adam from their loins,"* and [asked], *"Am I not your Lord?"* and they bore witness, *"Yea, we do bear witness..."* so that they not respond on the Day of Judgment by saying, *"We were unaware of this."* (7:173) Through this covenant, the human being becomes the trustee or representative of God on earth, accepts the trust of nature, and psychoethics is born.

SEEKING DIVINE ASSISTANCE

In order to carry out the duties of the trusteeship, Divine Assistance [2] is sought. It is always available if sought as the Sign says that God turns to those who turn to Him. (see 2:160). Algazel (d. 1111)[3] goes so far as to say that without Divine Assistance, there is no conscious communication between the Creator and the trustee. In other words, without consciousness of self, communication of the regulations of the trust remains indirect and preconscious or even, perhaps, unconscious. Algazel defines Divine Assistance as "the harmony, agreement, or concord of the self's will and action with God's Will." [4] It appears as a Sign,"*That is the Grace of God, a free gift which He gives to Whom He Wills,*" (5:54)[5] and consists of four stages: Guidance from God (*hidayah*), Direction (*rushd*), Leading (*tasdid*), and Confirmation (*ta'yid*).Guidance from God is of two types: guidance through nature (*takwini*) and guidance through nurture (*tashri'i*).

The Sign *"[God] gave unto everything its nature and further gave it guidance,"* (20:50) according to the traditional perspective, indicates God as the Creator and the Guide of all nature. Guidance is of two types, as previously stated. The first is *takwini* or primordial, universal guidance which all of nature receives, human or otherwise, as part of their *fitrat* or natural disposition. Universal guidance regulates whatever is created in nature through a natural,

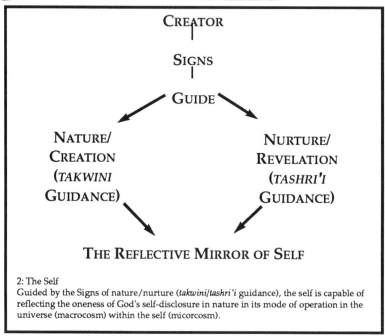

2: The Self
Guided by the Signs of nature/nurture (*takwini*/*tashri'i* guidance), the self is capable of reflecting the oneness of God's self-disclosure in nature in its mode of operation in the universe (macrocosm) within the self (micorcosm).

unreflective process, to implementing God's Will. Algazel expands on this type of guidance by saying, "He guides the young bird to pick up seeds from the time of its hatching; He guides the bee to build its house in a hexagonal form..." (fig. 2).

Human nature in the traditional perspective holds within itself all that came before it in creation, not in material terms, but in terms of "nature in its mode of operation,"[6] which is part of *takwini* guidance. Mineral, plant, animal, and human "souls" each contribute to a part of the development and perfection of nature's mode of operation. Minerals contribute preservation of the forms of the four elements of earth, air, fire, and water and their properties of cold and dry, hot and wet, hot and dry, and cold and wet, respectively. The plant soul contributes the ability to assimilate food, to grow, and to reproduce and the animal soul contributes perception and motivation.

At the time of the evolution of the human soul or self, nature in its mode of operation was completed with what is known as the infusion of the Divine Spirit. This became the human "self" which was given a uniquely original gift, as had each of the other stages of nature's evolution received, but for the self, the last offspring of creation, the gift was that of the capacity for consciousness as part of its natural disposition, a gift that it shares only with the Creator because of the covenant it made with God and the acceptance of the trust of nature.

The second type of both internal and external guidance is *tashri'i* or acquired guidance, referring to guidance through the commands of revelation. It is rational in orientation and therefore the special guidance of the human being alone. If accepted as guidance in the perspective of "submission to the Will of God" (*islam*), acquired guidance becomes yet another gift to one who actually does "submit to the Will of God" (*muslim*). It is a particular kind of guidance, in a sense, because it speaks to human consciousness. It is to elucidate this kind of guidance that God sends Prophets[7] and the Divine Law as reinforcement against the forgetful and negligent human beings declaring on the Day of Judgment, *"We were unaware of this."* (7:173)

Guidance acquired through revelation as a stage of Divine Grace or Assistance is considered to be a free gift from God because the giving was not obligatory on His part. However, the great theologian and philosopher, Algazel makes an important distinction here. God's communication through revelation, by which the self can acquire guidance, helps the self know the positive traits of its divinely bestowed natural disposition, but does not make the self actualize them through practices. The "self" is free to make the choice to follow *tashri'i* guidance or not to do so. If this guidance is not so chosen, the self will still be guided by *takwini* guidance, just as the rest of nature is. However, mineral, plant, and other animal forms have no choice, no free-will, so they submit completely to His Will in completing their stage of perfection of nature in its mode of operation.

A natural being that has consciousness, which relies solely on *takwini* guidance, will not succeed in "submitting to the Will of God" and completing the perfection of nature in its mode of operation because without the *tashri'i* guidance of revelation, there will be no strengthening of free-will through Divine Assistance of Direction, Leading, and Confirmation. These forms of Divine Assistance, along with Guidance from God, strengthen the will of the self so that it gains greater conformity to God's Will. Without Divine Assistance, choices will be made whereby one's mineral, plant, and animal nature will be strengthened as opposed to free-will following the advice of reason. In other words, without the guidance of the Prophets and the Divine Law, which are part of revelation, the self will live by guidance through creation alone, never learning to be able to achieve its full potential and never completing the perfection of nature in its mode of operation which God so Willed when He infused the Spirit into the human form.

Tashri'i guidance enhances the natural disposition of human conscience and power of discernment to know the difference between positive and negative dispositions. It also helps the human being regulate the states of the "self" at every level of change and transformation towards completing the perfection of nature in its mode of operation at its highest level. Algazel refers to the Sign, *"But to those who follow [tashri'i] guidance, He increases their guidance and bestows on them piety."*[8] (47:17)

Nasir al-Din Tusi (d. 1201) explains how guidance comes either through nature or discipline.

An example of nature is the principle which moves the passage of the sperm, through the degrees of transformations to the point where it reaches the perfection of an animal; an example of discipline is the principle which moves wood, by means of tools and instruments, to the point where it reaches the perfection of a couch. Since the perfection of any thing lies in the assimilation of that thing to its own principle, so the perfection of discipline (regulated by *tashri'i* guidance) lies in its assimilation to nature (*takwini* guidance). Its assimilation to nature means that it follows nature in the advancement or the relegation of causes, in putting everything in its place, and in the observance of gradation and classification so that the perfection towards which Divine Omnipotence has directed nature, by way of subjection, may be realized from discipline by way of regulation.[9]

> *TAKWINI* AND *TASHRI'I* GUIDANCE
>
> PERFECTION OF DISCIPLINE (BEING REGULATED BY *TASHRI'I* GUIDANCE) LIES IN ITS ASSIMILATION TO NATURE (*TAKWINI* GUIDANCE).
>
> *FOLLOWS NATURE IN ORDER TO ADVANCE ITS CAUSES
>
> *PUTS EVERYTHING IN ITS PLACE
>
> *OBSERVES GRADATIONS OF NATURE

In addition to Guidance from God in both its *takwini* and *tashri'i* forms, Divine Assistance contains three other previously eluded to stages, namely Direction (*rushd*), Leading (*tasdid*), and Confirmation (*ta'yid*). Direction (*rushd*), corresponds to the Divine Name which (*Rashid*) means "one who gives direction to all people in proportion to their acceptance of (*tashri'i*) guidance." [10] The Sign, *"And We verily gave Abraham of old his direction and were aware of him,"* (21:15) supports this stage of Divine Assistance which is present when the "self" senses it is being directed towards [*tashri'i*] guidance. When the self is aware of the fact that its will and actions together are directed to the right goal, its actions are made easier so that it achieves its goal in the shortest time possible and this is the third stage referred to by Algazel as Leading (*tasdid*). The final stage of Divine Assistance is Confirmation (*ta'yid*) which is referred to by the Sign, *"How I confirmed you with the Spirit,"* (5:113) which is present in the self when insight is strengthened inwardly while outwardly suitable conditions are provided within the means available to attain the goal.

The self is guided through *tashri'i* guidance to various methods available to it to prepare itself as part of its trust to receive Divine Assistance. The methods are among the Signs in the form of commands which are classified by Algazel according to the type of relationship the command refers. Algazel mentions two types of relationships for the trustee of nature as representative of God on earth to establish: first, the relationship between the self and its Creator-Guide; second, the relationship between self and one's fellow human beings.

ESTABLISHING THE RELATIONSHIP
BETWEEN THE SELF AND ITS CREATOR-GUIDE

This relationship is established, according to Algazel, through the commands of worship (*ibadah*), the most fundamental means of communication between the self and God, which are of two types: knowledge and actions. One who submits to the Will of God seeks knowledge of *tashri'i* guidance through revelation and then puts the knowledge so gained into actions.

KNOWLEDGE

According to Algazel, knowledge should be used to come to understand the articles of belief rather than accepting them on faith alone. The articles of belief include: the belief that God is One; the belief that God sent Prophets to guide mankind to Him and that Muhammad (ص) is the Messenger and last Prophet who will be sent until the end of time when Jesus (ع) will return and that the Quran is the last revelation; that after death the human being will be resurrected in the hereafter and judged by God who will reward or punish the person depending upon deeds performed in this life.

ACTIONS

The second type of commands that one who submits to the Will of God follows in seeking Divine Assistance in establishing the relationship between self and God concerns the actual performance of the major pillars of Islam. Knowledge alone is not sufficient for the self who accepted the trusteeship of nature and was endowed with the Divine Spirit which includes its abilities to choose, to discern, and to gain consciousness of self. It is through actions based on knowledge that the centered self benefits another as proof of being centered. The major pillars include ritual purity (taharah) and ritual prayer (salah), ritual fast (saum), the paying of the alms tax (zakah), the pilgrimage (hajj), counseling to positive dispositions and preventing the development of negative ones (amr bi'l ma'ruf wa nahy an al-munkar) and jihad or struggle in the Way of God, the greater struggle of which is the inward struggle of the self (jihad al-akbar). The last two are the major concern of psychoethics.

As a result of the performance of these acts of worship, if accompanied by Divine Assistance, the one who submits to the Will of God will be receptive to the adoption of positive dispositions like temperance, courage, wisdom, and justice and be able to avoid negative dispositions like anger, fear of other than God, cowardice, lust, envy, apathy, preconsciousness (knowing that you do not know), unconsciousness (not knowing that you do not know) and overconsciousness (knowing but deceiving the self about it), but only on the condition that others benefit from the positive dispositions one has attained. This, then, makes it encumbent on the one who has submitted to the Will of God to come to know and act upon the commands that underlie the relationship of self to others.

ESTABLISHING THE RELATIONSHIP
BETWEEN THE SELF AND OTHERS

These commands give a framework for the establishment of the relationship between self and others including all social, political, and economic affairs undertaken among human beings. The model for all of this is the *sunnah* of Muhammad (ﷺ) who said, "I was sent to complete the noble qualities of dispositions," explaining that God loves the positive dispositions and not the negative ones.[11] Algazel also quotes another Tradition in this regard, "By Him in whose hand is my life, no one shall enter paradise except the one who has positive dispositions."[12] Algazel says, "God taught [Muhammad (ﷺ)] all the fine qualities of disposition, praiseworthy paths, reports about the first and last affairs, and matters through which one achieves salvation and reward in future life and happiness and reward in the world to come."[13] Among the qualities listed are thirty obligations that one who submits has towards another (fig. 6).[14]

This process of the *sunnah* whereby the positive dispo-

sitions of wisdom, temperance, and courage are kept in
moderation resulting in the development of the positive
trait of justice is the traditional method of "centering the
self" and it begins by becoming conscious of self, "knowing self."[15]

KNOW THE SELF

The establishment of any of the relationships, according to Algazel, begins with gaining knowledge of one's
self.

Know that the key to knowledge of
God is knowledge of one's self. That is
why it has been said, 'One who knows
one's own 'self,' knows one's Lord.'
That is also why God said, 'We shall
show them Our Signs upon the horizons
and within themselves until it is clear to
them that He is the Real.' (41:53) In
short, nothing is closer to you than
you. If you do not know your 'self,'
how will you know others? Moreover,
you may think that you know your
'self' and be mistaken, for this kind of
knowing is not the key to the knowledge of the Real. The beasts know this
much of themselves—since of your
'self' you know no more than the outward head, face, hands, feet, flesh, and
skin. Of the inward dimension you
know that when you are hungry, you
eat bread, and when you are angry, you
fall on the other person, and when
'attraction to pleasure' dominates, you
make for the marriage act. All the
beasts know that much. Hence you

PROPHETIC TRADITION

"ONE WHO KNOWS
ONE'S OWN 'SELF',
KNOWS ONE'S LORD."

**QUESTIONS TO
ASK THE SELF:**
WHO ARE YOU?
FROM WHENCE HAVE YOU
COME?
WHY WERE YOU CREATED?
WHAT AND WHERE IS
YOUR FELICITY?
WHAT AND FROM WHERE
LIES
YOUR MISERY?

> ## SELF CONSISTS OF OUTWARD FRAME
> ### AND
> ## INWARD MEANING
>
> ALGAZEL:
> "YOUR REALITY IS THAT INWARD MEANING. EVERYTHING ELSE FOLLOWS UPON IT."

must seek your own reality. What thing are you? From whence have you come? Where will you go? For what work have you come to this dwelling place? Why were you created? What and where is your felicity? What and from where lies your misery?

If you want to know your 'self,' you should know that when you were created, two things were created: one is this outward frame, which is called the body. It can be seen with the outward eye. The second is the inward meaning which is called the self (or the soul), the spirit, and the heart. It can be recognized through inward insight but cannot be seen with the outward eye. Your reality is that inward meaning. Everything else follows upon it. [16]

Beginning with the "self" and moving towards centering it by completing the perfection of nature in its mode of operation is to submit to God's Will (*islam*), thereby attaining happiness and well-being (*sa'adat*). It is an arduous task in which many who have attempted have not succeeded (figs. 3, 4, 5).

> COME YOU LOST ATOMS,
> TO YOUR CENTER DRAW
> AND BE THE ETERNAL MIRROR
> THAT YOU SAW:
> RAYS THAT HAVE WANDERED
> INTO DARKNESS WIDE
> RETURN AND BACK INTO
> YOUR SUN SUBSIDE.
>
> 3: Farid al-Din Attar, *Mantiq al-Tayr*.

> THE VISIBLE WORLD
> WAS MADE TO CORRESPOND
> TO THE WORLD INVISIBLE
> AND THERE IS
> NOTHING IN THIS WORLD
> BUT IS A SYMBOL
> OF SOMETHING
> IN THAT OTHER WORLD.
>
> 4: Algazel, *Ihya*, in Margaret Smith, *al-Ghazali, the Mystic*, p. 111.

GOD'S WILL BE DONE:
THE PRIMORDIAL GOAL OF THE SELF

The human being, then, is the trustee of creation, the human spirit at the time of its first creation having agreed to the terms of the trusteeship. Following the commands of God's Signs in nature and within themselves[17] the human being is responsible to carry out God's Will so that all of nature be allowed to "center itself" by completing the perfection of nature in its mode of operation as a Sign says, *"He gave unto everything its nature, and further, gave it guidance."* (20:50) Everything in nature but the human "self" perfects its own nature, to the extent that life allows, by unconsciously submitting to the Will of God and the study of this is the concern of the Natural Sciences.

The area with which psychoethics is concerned is the completion of the perfection of nature in its mode of operation through centering in positive dispositions. Having ethically formed the covenant and accepted the trust, God breathed His Spirit into human forms so that they gained the powers of consciousness of self which includes freely choosing positive dispositions from negative ones by consciously following one's conscience. The completion of the perfection of nature in its mode of operation, as God so willed, as opposed to all other natural forms, then, becomes a question of choice—to do or not to do.

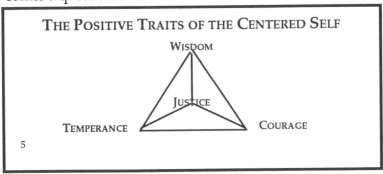

THE POSITIVE TRAITS OF THE CENTERED SELF

WISDOM

JUSTICE

TEMPERANCE   COURAGE

5

A TRADITION OF THE PROPHET:

30 OBLIGATIONS

ON ALL BELIEVERS TOWARDS THEIR BROTHERS AND SISTERS

1 FORGIVING THEIR MISTAKES

2 BEING MERCIFUL TO THEM WHEN THEY ARE IN A STRANGE LAND

3 GUARDING THEIR SECRETS

4 GIVING THEM A HAND WHEN ABOUT TO FALL

5 ACCEPTING THEIR APOLOGIES

6 DISCOURAGING BACKBITING ABOUT THEM

7 PERSISTING IN GIVING THEM GOOD ADVICE

8 TREASURING THEIR FRIENDSHIP

9 FULFILLING THEIR TRUSTS

10 VISITING THEM WHEN THEY ARE ILL

11 BEING WITH THEM AT THE TIME OF THEIR DEATH

12 ACCEPTING THEIR INVITATION AND THEIR PRESENTS

13 RETURNING THEIR FAVORS IN KIND

14 THANKING THEM FOR THEIR FAVORS

15 BEING GRATEFUL FOR THEIR ASSISTANCE

16 PROTECTING THEIR HONOR AND PROPERTY

17 HELPING THEM MEET THEIR NEEDS

18 MAKING AN EFFORT TO SOLVE THEIR PROBLEMS

19 GUIDING THEM TO THE THINGS THEY HAVE LOST

20 ANSWERING THEIR GREETINGS

21 TAKING THEM AT THEIR WORD

22 ACCEPTING THEIR BESTOWALS

23 CONFIRMING THEM IF THEY SWEAR TO SOMETHING

24 BEING KIND AND FRIENDLY TOWARDS THEM

25 HELPING THEM WHEN THEY ARE BEING UNJUST

26 HELPING THEM WHEN THEY ARE A VICTIM OF INJUSTICE

27 REFRAINING FROM FEELING BORED WITH THEM

28 NOT FORSAKING THEM IN TIMES OF TROUBLE

29 WHATEVER GOOD YOU LIKE, LIKE FOR THEM

30 WHATEVER EVIL YOU DISLIKE, DISLIKE FOR THEM

Psychoethics plays a central role in this process. Naraqi (d. 1893) explains how all of the other sciences were dependent upon this pivotal one:

PSYCHOETHICS IS THE BASIS OF ALL SCIENCES

In fact, in the past, philosophers did not consider any of the other fields of learning to be truly independent sciences. They believed that without the science of psychoethics, mastery over any other science is not only devoid of any value, but it would, in fact, lead to the obstruction of insight and ultimate destruction of those who pursue it. That is why it has been said that knowledge is the thickest of veils which prevents the human being from seeing the real nature of things. [18]

CONCLUSION

Psychoethics arises out of the Science of Ethics, a branch of practical philosophy which is concerned with free-will actions of the self. The self is considered to be the highest evolutionary form of nature in its mode of operation because it has received the special Divine Gift of consciousness, a gift arising out of the Divine Spirit infused within the children of Adam. It was given when the human being made the covenant with God and accepted the trust of nature. As trustee of the Creator, the human being alone is responsible for the trusteeship which includes completing the perfection of nature in its mode of operation. Laws governing nature in its mode of operation are expressed through Signs that appear on the horizon and within the self. The self has access to the language of the Signs through two kinds of guidance: *takwini*—universal to all of nature—and *tashri'i*— special guidance for human consciousness alone. Learning to read the Signs on the horizon and within the self is a task undertaken by the only one who consciously submits to the Will of God. Committed to the completion of the perfection of nature in its mode of operation, the self seeks Divine Assistance.

In order for the trustee to perform the trust, and complete the perfection of nature in its mode of operation, it should begin with knowing self, awakening to the self as it really is, becoming conscious of self including the development of the *takwini* guided conscience and free-will. In order to further this goal, psychoethics formulates the geography or topography of the self; its structure or morphology; and its dynamics (fig. 7).

NOTES TO OVERVIEW

1 See Algazel (Ghazali), *Ihya*, III, 22, 18 where the story originated. Also see the *Mathnawi* of Jalal al-Din Rumi, I. 3467 where the roles are reversed because his audience was in Asia Minor.

The author uses the Latinized names throughout this work of those Muslim scholars known to the West for two reasons: first, in order to call recognition to their influence upon the development of Western thought and second, in order to further understanding between the three great monotheistic faiths who all worship the same God and have many similarities in belief system. A summary of the relevance of the scholars quoted in this work to psychoethics can be found in the glossary.

Also, the translations used throughout this work are a combination of this author and the book as referred to in the bibliography unless otherwise indicated. Page numbers refer to the original. For Algazel, see Glossary.

2 The author gratefully acknowledges the work of M. M. Sharif and M. A. Sherif for the development of this section.

3 Algazel, *al-Mizan*, p. 115.

4 Algazel, *Ihya Ulum al-Din*, IV, 2.2255.

5 See also 3:73, 57:29, 3:171, 3:174, 49:8.

6 This is traditionally referred to as the 'soul'.

7 Although all of the Prophets of the Old Testament and the Prophet Jesus (ε) are considered to have been human beings who in the most excellent way submitted to God's Will and completed the perfection of their divinely-bestowed human nature, it is His Last Prophet in time, Muhammad (ص), known as the Seal of the Prophets, who is the main model of one who submits to His Will because his every word and deed was recorded during his actual lifetime and therefore his example has greater reality as a model.

8 Algazel also identifies a further stage of guidance as "the light which illuminates," but this is a form beyond reason and rationality and therefore is discussed in *Jihad Phase II*. He refers to two Signs in reference to it, namely, *"Say: God's guidance is the guidance,"* (6:71) and *"Whenever God wills to guide a human being,*

He enlarges his breast for surrender [to Him] (islam)." (6:125)
9 Tusi, p. 115. For Tusi, see Glossary.
10 Algazel, *Maqsad*, p. 97.
11 Algazel, *Ihya Ulum al-Din*, Vol. 2, p. 10.
12 *Ibid.*, Vol. 2, p. 10.
13 *Ibid.*, Vol. 2, p. 10.
14 *Ibid.*, Vol. 2, p. 10.
15 The theory, process, and mechanics of this are developed in *Jihad Phase I: Centering the Self.*
16 For the translation see McCarthy, *Freedom and Fulfillment.*
17 This implies that all of nature is sacred and that it is the human being who creates profanities.
18 Naraqi, p. 45. For Naraqi, see Glossary.

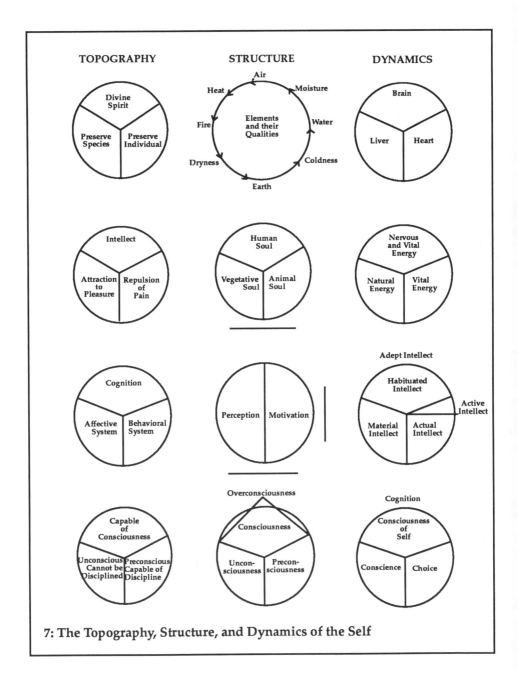

7: The Topography, Structure, and Dynamics of the Self

NATURE IN ITS MODE OF OPERATION IN THE SELF

DEVELOPMENTAL LEVELS

GOD'S SELF-DISCLOSURE:

CREATOR

CLAY COMBINATION OF:

ELEMENTS/
MINERALS
{ EARTH/COLD AND DRY
WATER/COLD AND MOIST
FIRE/HOT AND DRY
AIR/HOT AND MOIST

PLANTS { NUITRITIVE, GROWTH, AND REPRODUCTION FUNCTIONS

ANIMALS { PERCEPTION AND MOTIVATION

+ DIVINE SPIRIT

HUMANS { COGNITION

PHYSIOLOGICAL LEVELS

ENERGY SYSTEMS FOR THE DYNAMICS OF SELF

NERVOUS SYSTEM

ARTERIES

VEINS

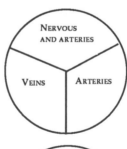

ORGANS

BRAIN

HEART

LIVER (GUT)

SHOWN AS IF THE SELF IS WITHIN THE CIRCLE LOOKING
OUT TO MIRROR THE UNIVERSE SO THAT THE HEART IS ON
THE LEFT FROM WITHIN AND ON THE RIGHT FROM WITH-
OUT. THE SAME IS TRUE OF THE LIVER (GUT).

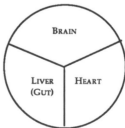

PART I:
TRADITIONAL
PERSONALITY
PARADIGM

NATURE IN ITS MODE OF OPERATION
PSYCHOLOGICAL LEVELS

DISPOSITIONS: MOST BASIC, NATURAL
    DIVINE SPIRIT
      PRESERVE THE INDIVIDUAL
      PRESERVE THE SPECIES

FUNCTIONS: MOST BASIC, NATURAL
    PERCEPTION
      EXTERNAL SENSES
      INTERNAL SENSES
      CONSCIENCE
    MOTIVATION
      ATTRACTION TO PLEASURE
      REPULSION OF HARM/PAIN
      FREE-WILL

SYSTEMS: MOST BASIC
    COGNITIVE
    BEHAVIORAL
    AFFECTIVE/EMOTIVE

COGNITION: MOST BASIC
    CAPABLE OF CONSCIOUSNESS
    PRECONSCIOUSNESS
    UNCONSCIOUSNESS

1

2
TOPOGRAPHY

THE TRADITIONAL CONCEPT OF SELF

The soul/self is one single substance capable of a multiplicity of operations (fig. 1). In terms of operations, it is the internal cause of life, motivation, perception, and understanding. Seen as the process of nature in its mode of operation, the soul is called self in the human form. This distinction is made because in all of creation, only the human form holds the possibility of attaining consciousness of self; only the human form has accepted the trust of nature; only the human form has been infused with the Divine Spirit. It is this latter aspect of the self which is considered to be immortal thereby surviving the death of the physical form. This means that it will be held accountable on the Day of Judgment and rewarded and punished according to a person's intentions, words, and deeds.

Philosophical arguments are given as to why this is so. In regard to its incorporeality, to its possessing an existence independent of the body, and to its immateriality, Naraqi says:

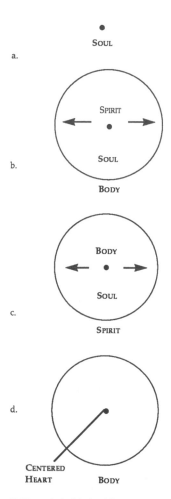

a.

SOUL

SPIRIT

← • →

SOUL

b.

BODY

BODY

← • →

SOUL

c.

SPIRIT

d.

CENTERED
HEART   BODY

2: Nature in its Mode of Operation

First of all, one of the characteristics of bodies is that whenever any forms and shapes are imposed upon them, they renounce and abandon their previous forms or shapes. In the self, however, new forms, whether of the sensible or of the intellectual nature, enter continuously without wiping out the previously existing forms. In fact, the more impressions and intellectual forms enter the mind, the stronger does the self become. Second, when three elements of color, smell, and taste appear in an object, it is transformed. The self, however, perceives all of these conditions without being materially affected by them. Third, the pleasures that the human being experiences from intellectual cognition can belong only to the self since the body plays no role in it. Fourth, abstract forms and concepts which are perceived by the mind are undoubtedly non-material and indivisible. Accordingly, their vehicle, which is the self, must also be indivisible and therefore immaterial. Fifth, the physical faculties of the human being receive their input through the senses, while the self perceives certain things without the help of the senses. Among the things that the self comprehends without relying on the senses are the law of contradiction, the idea that the whole is always greater than the sum of its parts, and other such universal principles. The negation of the errors made by the senses on the part of the self, such as optical illusions, is done with the aid of these abstract concepts, even though the raw material required for making corrections is provided by the senses.[1]

3: Jihad Phase II

Various terms are used to describe the self: heart (*qalb*), soul (*nafs*), spirit (*ruh*), and intellect ('*aql*) (fig. 2a, b, c, d). Each of these can be discussed in its material and spiritual aspect. Although different in terms of meaning, the spiritual sense of each of these terms refers to the same entity, the self, but different spiritually transformed states of it. At the level of centering, only those aspects referred to as intellect and soul are included as Phase I of the inner, "Greater Jihad." Phase II (fig. 3) is concerned with those aspects of self as referred to as heart and spirit. This phase begins after the self is centered when it then begins to spiral on the return to its Source.

The self has more value than the body in the traditional perspective because of the very infusion in the self of the potential of consciousness which is a subtle, non-material phenomenon whereas the body, the physical form, is created from earth or "putrid clay." The self, therefore, the essence of what can be called "human being," can only be known, understood, and studied indirectly with the cognitive power of reason and deliberation observing the activities that originate from it. In the traditional perspective, this refers to the states and activities of the self and how transformation occurs from not knowing to knowing.

Nasir al-Din Tusi describes the subject of psychoethics and the process whereby the self can attain its primordial goal of the completion of the perfection of nature in its mode of operation.

WHAT IS THE SELF?
WHERE DOES ITS
PERFECTION LIE?
WHAT ARE THE
FUNCTIONS
OF THE SELF, IF USED IN
MODERATION, HELP
IT ATTAIN WHAT IT SEEKS?
WHAT PREVENTS IT FROM
REACHING PERFECTION?
HOW IS THE SELF
PURIFIED?
HOW IS THE SELF
SEDUCED?

The subject matter of this science, then, is the human 'self' in as much as from it can proceed, according to its free-will, acts fair and praiseworthy or negative and destructive. This being so, it must be known what the self is, where its perfection lies, what the functions are by which, if used in moderation, it attains what it seeks, namely perfection of nature [in its method of operation] and what prevents it from reaching that perfection. In other words, one needs to know how to purify the 'self' and avoid seducing it, thereby bringing about its prosperity rather than its failure. As the Quran says, *"By the self and that which shaped it and inspired it with wickedness and godfearing. Prospered is the one who purifies it and failed is one who seduces it."* (91:7-10)[2]

The "self" (fig. 4) in the traditional perspective consists of three major systems: affective (preserve the species; attraction to pleasure), behavioral (preserve the individual; avoidance of harm/pain), and cognitive (fig. 1).

Suppose that you are in a state of crisis because your mother, whom you loved a great deal, has just died and the impulse of grief and sadness is so great that it overcomes you. This is the affective/emotive system at work in a naturally unbalanced state. You can either stay cognitively unconscious with the grief to the point that it effects your physical state as well or become cognitively conscious of its effects upon you whereby you try to consciously regulate it through free-will and conscience. In the latter case, little by little you motivate the self to perceive the situation as negative because of the effect that it

4: Topography

is having on you. You are then able to face life and avoid the harm that the grief is causing you. This is the cognitive system working on the behavioral system which responds by gaining courage. You begin to tell yourself that everyone has to die at some point and start to remember the positive traits of your mother and you begin to recall the sacrifices she made for you. This is the cognitive system consciously at work, regulating the affective and behavioral systems.

THE AFFECTIVE SYSTEM

The affective/emotive or "attraction to pleasure" system is the most basic of the three systems which evolved out of the animal stage of nature in its mode of operation. At birth it potentially contains all of the systems necessary to transform energy in order to preserve the species as it is naturally disposed to do. As life unfolds and one responds to inner impulses and outer stimuli with affect, "attracting pleasure," it is the potential energy of this system which is being used. The affective system is considered to be naturally disposed to unconsciousness to such a degree that it is incapable of being disciplined by the cognitive system even if the cognitive system is in balance in consciousness.

The cognitive system in balance can only regulate the unconscious, affective system. Otherwise, the affective system dominates the self (fig. 5). In terms of psychoethics, completion of the perfection of nature in its mode of operation in the affective system is to attain the positive disposition of temperance.

THE BEHAVIORAL SYSTEM

The second system to be generated in the human being, which is still close to its animal nature at this point, is the behavioral or "avoidance of pain" system. Again, this aspect of self is shared with other animals and at birth potentially contains all the systems necessary to transform energy towards its natural disposition to preserve the individual. As one grows, responding to inner impulses and outer stimuli which cause impulses to generate from the energy source of the behavioral system, one responds in defense of the self to avoid pain/harm. The behavioral system is considered to be in a preconscious state in the sense that it is capable of learning discipline and modifying itself if regulated by a balanced cognitive system (fig. 5). As regards psychoethics, completion of the perfection of nature in its mode of operation in the behavioral system is the development of the positive disposition of courage.

THE AFFECTIVE/EMOTIVE
AND BEHAVIORAL SYSTEMS

The affective-behavioral systems are known in the Quran as *nafs al-ammarah* or animal soul, neither of these two systems can attain consciousness. Often referred to as "the passions" or irrational systems in philosophy and theology, they can corrupt the rational system and seduce free-will. They arise out of the internal sense of imagination and through inner impulses to move the self to attracting pleasures or avoiding harms. The motion that they cause initially is referred to as emotion. Although they are analyzed as two separate tendencies, they are actually different tendencies of the single self.

The affective system, according to psychoethics, attracts love and pleasures while the behavioral system avoids hate and pain. Although both are located in the heart, the affective system receives its energies from the organ of the liver through the veins to attract to pleasure. It is the most basic drive of human nature. The behavioral system, on the other hand, receives its energies from that of the heart through the arteries. The two together, therefore, act to "attract pleasure" and "avoid pain or harm" (fig. 6).

Rhazes describes the relationship of pleasure and pain and how the natural state of the self is one of pleasure.

Pleasure consists simply of the restoration of that condition which was expelled by the element of pain, while passing from one's actual state until one returns to the state formerly experienced. An example is provided by the man who leaves a restful, shady spot to go out into the desert; there he proceeds under the summer sun until he is affected by the heat; then he returns to his former place. He continues to feel pleasure in that place, until his body returns to its original state; then he loses the sense of pleasure as his body goes back to normal. The intensity of his pleasure on coming home is in proportion to the degree of intensity of the heat and the speed of his cooling-off in that place. Hence the philosophers have defined pleasure as a return to the state of nature.

SIGNS OF THE PSYCHOETHICAL STATES OF THE AFFECTIVE SYSTEM
(*) TEMPERANCE, MODESTY
(O) ENVY, GRIEF
(+) GREED, GLUTTONY
(-) APATHY, MISERLINESS

SIGNS OF THE PSYCHOETHICAL STATES OF THE BEHAVIORAL SYSTEM
(*) COURAGE, GENTLENESS
(O) FEAR OF OTHER THAN GOD
(+) ANGER, CONCEIT
(-) COWARDICE, INFERIORITY COMPLEX

5: Signs or dispositions can be considered positive or negative. The positive sign is indicated by (*). Negative signs may indicate an imbalance in quantity as an overdevelopment (+) or underdevelopment (-). Imbalance in quality appears in the self as undevelopment (o).

SIGNS OF
PSYCHOTHEICAL
DISORDERS OF THE
COMBINED AFFECTIVE/
BEHAVIORAL
SYSTEMS

*Jealousy

*Degrading others

*Sticking nose in
others business

*Causing friction
among people

*Backbiting

*Lying

*Coveting fame

*Anxiety

Now since pain and the departure from the state of nature sometimes occur little by little over a long period of time, and then the return to the state of nature happens all at once, in a brief space, under such circumstances we are not aware of the element of pain, whereas the sharpness of the sense of a return to nature is multiplied. This state we call pleasure. Those who have had no training suppose this has happened without any prior pain; they imagine it is a pure and solitary phenomenon, wholly disassociated from pain. Now this is not really the case at all; there cannot in fact be any pleasure except in proportion to a prior pain, that of departing from the state of nature. One takes pleasure in eating and drinking according to the degree to which one has hungered and thirsted; when the hungry and thirsty person returns to his original state, there is no more worse torture than to compel him to go on partaking of food and drink, in spite of the fact that just previously he could think of nothing more pleasurable and desirable than these. It is the same with all other pleasures: the definition is universally valid and all-embracing. [3]

Thus, the natural state is one of pleasure whether it be in attracting pleasures (preserving the species) or in protecting the pleasure system (preserving the species) by avoiding harm/pain (preserving the individual). If either of these two systems are regulated by a balanced cognitive system, the self is in balance. If the affective dominates, the self is attracted to all sorts of pleasures. If the behavioral system dominates, the self is ruled by the urge for power and ambition.

These two systems cooperate in such a way that the actions of the behavioral system unite with or replace those of affect whenever the self is in difficulty. When an object has been perceived as desirable, affection responds, and from this, in turn, the desire to possess it. If the object can easily be procured, the affective/attraction to pleasure system supplies sufficient energy. However, if any obstacles get in the way, the behavioral/avoidance of pain system yields hope in support of the affective system, enabling the self to strive with great effort to effect the purpose of the affective system. It may deprive the self of contentment until the difficulty has been overcome. Whenever there is an insurmountable problem, the affective system is overwhelmed with loss of hope so that energy is not spent in vain.

The same is true in regard to avoidance of pain. Courage leads the self to combat that which oppresses it and fear prevents its persisting against great odds. Whenever difficulty afflicts the self, the behavioral system supports the affective.

The result is far more dangerous to the balance of the self than when they each act alone. The behavioral system may induce the self to pursue that which is contrary to the affective system. It may risk its very life to seek revenge. Thus the very means which nature in its mode of operation provided to insure the survival of the individual may prove its undoing. The two systems, acting together, fan into a flame that destroys rationality.

The affective-behavioral systems may proceed from a mild state to an extreme one. Desire of a future good kindles hope or despair. The resentment of a future event stirs fear or courage. The perception of a present evil, which at first caused grief, may incite anger. The progress between the two is frequently from grief to anger.

If these two systems dominate, they blind understanding. Like looking through rose colored glasses, everything appears "rosy." They can cause reason to judge whatever promotes their needs as good and agreeable to reason. Their domination can be so strong that the energies of the self are exhausted and their perception, then, prevents the self from returning to a normal state.

Other characteristics of affective response to a situation include contradiction, contrariety, insatiability, importunity, and impossibility. Contradiction and contrariety have to do with reason. When the self least expects it, the two systems may completely undermine rationality. While it is engaged in thought, a motion so strong may creep into the heart that the self is carried beyond all control. The desires of these systems neither keep order or measure because of their incapacity for reflection.

THE COGNITIVE SYSTEM

Up to this point the human being in traditional psychology is akin to the animal. If the evolution of the human self did not proceed beyond this, the human form would just be another of the animal species. The difference lies in the third system of the personality or self that lies within the cognitive system.

The cognitive system is naturally disposed to perception and motivation out of which evolve consciousness of self, the highest form of evolution of nature in its mode of operation. It is the center where knowledge is stored and actions initiate.

The cognitive system is actualized through nurture and its final form depends upon the quality and quantity of the environment in which the self grows and develops. If the nurturing process is a psychically healthy one, the self will actualize its natural disposition for discerning between positive and negative dispositions. This is done through the Will of the Creator flowing through nature in its mode of operation, which the self can accept or reject. Guided by nature/*takwini* and nurture/*tashri'i*, the self moves towards understanding God's Signs and positive dispositions. This is the process of preservation of psychic health. [4]

If the nurturing process is a psychically unhealthy one in terms of God's Will in nature in its mode of operation, the self will be led astray. In terms of free-will actions, an underdevelopment of this function is called a state of pre-consciousness, that is, not being present in consciousness, but capable of being "reminded" of it without encountering any resistance or repression, "knowing that you do not know." An undevelopment of this function, a negative trait which is known as the most fatal kind, is unconsciousness. Alienated from self-awareness, unconscious impulses are naturally disposed to be stronger to preserve the human race and the individual when there is no possibility of consciousness (exercise of free-will and conscience). It is not knowing and not knowing that you do not know. When there is an overdevelopment of this function, cleverness and identity disturbances take over the self.

If guidance comes at a later life stage, the self will then make the attempt to implement the Divine Will and perfect its God-given nature in its mode of operation. This is a process known as restoration of psychic health.[5] If not, the self will live out its life in a state of unconsciousness, unaware of its true potential, never completing the perfection of nature in its mode of operation.

DISPOSITIONS

Dispositions or states of being are both natural and acquired. Whether natural or acquired, either can be regulated by conscious or unconscious habits, habits being the continual repetition of certain acts.

Natural dispositions are never changed, in the sense that the original is lost, but rather, through nurturing, they can become hidden or concealed just as a mirror can lose its reflective capacity with the formation of rust, dust, or fog. The mirror is still there, but it reflects rust, dust, and fog rather than the its original, naturally disposed polished surface. Therefore, the natural disposition changes at the same time that it is always there and no energy is lost in the change.

The self is born with a natural disposition to meet physiological and psychoethical needs of the self. Psychoethical needs, which are part of the self's natural disposition, are positive aspects of nature in its mode of operation trying to perfect the "self." These form the mirror of self. The nurturing process clouds, distorts, and darkens this mirror, thereby distancing the self from its true nature. Change is effected through methods known as "polishing" or "purifying" the mirror of self so that it can once again reflect the positive aspects of nature with which it was naturally disposed.

Change, growth, and transformation in the traditional perspective do not mean that the natural disposition of reproduction or self-preservation should be repressed or suppressed because the human race could not exist without them. The point made in the traditions is that the mean and moderation, balance and equilibrium, are the norm so that all natural dispositions function properly. Naraqi then metaphorically explains,

The seed of a date grows into a fruitful tree through proper care or a wild horse is trained to serve his master, or a dog is trained to be the lifelong friend and help to the human being, [even more so] can the human being complete the perfection of nature in its mode of operation and gain wisdom through self-discipline and intelligent perseverance [because of the possibility of consciousness]. [6]

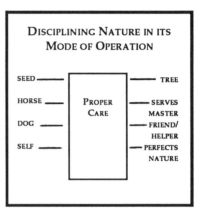

DISCIPLINING NATURE IN ITS MODE OF OPERATION

SEED ——— ——— TREE
HORSE ——— PROPER CARE ——— SERVES MASTER
DOG ——— ——— FRIEND/ HELPER
SELF ——— ——— PERFECTS NATURE

Dispositions are described as "that which is the source of all of the actions that the self undertakes spontaneously without thinking about them."[7] A natural disposition may be the result of natural and physical make-up by which the self is endowed at birth with what is known physiologically as temperament. Temperament arises from the combination of elemental qualities of hot-wet, hot-dry, cold-wet, and cold-dry which develop depending on the constellation of birth, the geographic location of the parents at the time of the intercourse which leads to conception, of a mother during the time of pregnancy, the food that each eats, and the air that each breathes. Even though temperament is natural, it can be changed, regulated, or neutralized as a disposition or psychological structure through the centering process (fig. 7).

TRAITS: POSITIVE AND NEGATIVE

A disposition that becomes embedded in the self is known as a trait. The self in the traditional perspective is created pure and good and starts life with a "clean slate," in the sense that it is free of negative traits. Negative traits develop through contact with one's environment—parents, family, friends, schooling, work, and so forth. These traits are directly related to the way a person lives and thinks and are reinforced by one's words and deeds and concealed if negative resulting from the lack of nuturing guidance. Penetrating through the self, traits become the origin and cause of human actions. Naraqi explains:

> **POSITIVE TRAITS ARE NOBLE**
> Self appears through moral and wise speech.
>
> **NEGATIVE TRAITS**
> Self appears through abnormal and disturbed behavior.

The self becomes used to these traits, joins them, and determines the self's direction in accordance with their dictates. If these traits are positive, they are considered to be noble. They manifest themselves as moral and wise speech and behavior in the self. If, on the contrary, they are negative, they are manifested through abnormal and disturbed behavior.[8]

When a negative disposition is reinforced through behavior, it becomes imbedded in the self as a trait which requires greater conscious effort on the part of the cognitive system to undo. Naraqi says:

NEGATIVE TRAITS DEVELOP THROUGH NURTURE AS SHADOWS OVER THE SELF

ACQUIRED TRAITS

NATURAL DISPOSITION

The thing to keep in mind is that when a negative disposition is reinforced through behavior, it leads to the development of a negative trait in the self. This negative trait, then, through habit becomes "stable" in the self and the punishment and torture which accompanies it will also afflict the self. The Quran says: *"And every man—We have fastened to him his bird of omen upon his neck; and We shall bring forth for him on the Day of Resurrection a book he shall find spread wide open. Read your book! Your soul suffices you this day as a reckoner against you."* (17:13-14) And *"The book shall be set in place; and you will see the sinners fearful at what is in it, saying, 'Alas for us how is it with this Book that it leaves nothing behind, small or great, but it has numbered it?' And they shall find all they brought present and your Lord shall not wrong anyone."* (18:49) And, *"The day every soul shall find what it has done of good brought forward and what it has done of evil; it will wish if there were only a far space between it and its deeds."* (3:29)[9]

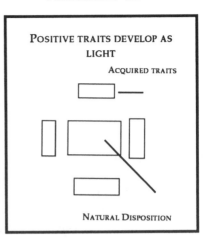

The purpose of psychoethics, then, is to first try to preserve the *fitrat* or natural disposition (s) of the self—which is called the healthy self— through the nurturing process.

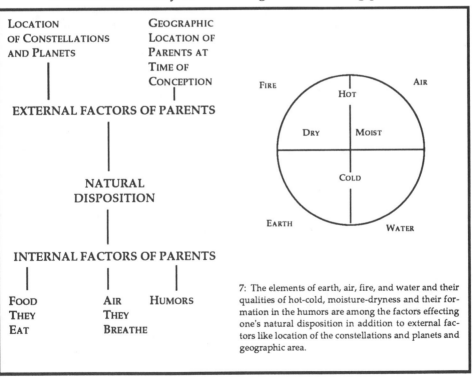

7: The elements of earth, air, fire, and water and their qualities of hot-cold, moisture-dryness and their formation in the humors are among the factors effecting one's natural disposition in addition to external factors like location of the constellations and planets and geographic area.

One of the methods of both preservation of one's natural disposition or restoration back to it is self-training and conscious effort to adopt positive habits. It has been shown through centuries of experience that this will lead to a positive disposition and the stabilization of positive traits resulting in a healthy self. Psychoethics and the methods of preservation of psychic health[10] and/or its restoration when an imbalance occurs, basically deal with the development of traits that are slow to decline. The "self" becomes centered when traits fall under the regula-

NATURE IN ITS MODE OF OPERATION
PSYCHOETHICAL LEVELS

WISDOM
INFUSED BY THE DIVINE SPIRIT
BRAIN
NERVOUS AND ARTERIES ENERGY SYSTEMS
INTELLECT
COGNITION
CAPABLE OF CONSCIOUSNESS

COURAGE
PRESERVE INDIVIDUAL
HEART
ARTERIAL ENERGY SYSTEM
AVOIDANCE OF HARM/PAIN
BEHAVIORAL SYSTEM
PRECONSCIOUSNESS

BRAIN

LIVER (GUT)

HEART

TEMPERANCE
PRESERVE SPECIES
LIVER (GUT)
VEINAL ENERGY SYSTEM
ATTRACTION TO PLEASURE
AFFECTIVE SYSTEM
UNCONSCIOUSNESS

JUSTICE
CENTERED IF:
RECEIVED DIVINE ASSISTANCE
ANOTHER BENEFITS
SELF REGULATED BY COGNITIVE SYSTEM

8

tion of cognition so that a positive disposition evolves.

The positive traits that indicate "centeredness" in psychoethics develop out of the previous three systems: affective, behavioral, and cognitive. The positive disposition of the affective system is temperance. The positive disposition of the behavioral system is courage. The positive disposition of the cognitive intellect is wisdom. When these three positive dispositions are in balance, regulated by the conscious cognitive system, the fourth positive disposition is attained, that of justice (fig. 8). These are the positive traits all of which appear in the Quran and the *sunnah*. They are chosen as the "mothers of character" from among the many positive traits mentioned because of the central role they play in the analysis of the self. They are distinguished by various functions therein. These four positive traits are also mentioned by Plato and Aristotle with a slight difference in values. They are accepted into the Islamic tradition by Algazel for two clear reasons: first of all, they are part of the Quran and the *sunnah*; and secondly they can be arrived at through the observation of nature. He says,

Nothing of what we have mentioned [from the Greek philosophers] need be denied on religious grounds, for all these things are observable facts whose habitual course has been provided by God." [11]

> "THE GREEKS OBSERVED THE HABITUAL COURSE OF GOD'S CREATION."
> —ALGAZEL

Therefore, these positive traits are part of the Signs of guidance which can be found in nature (*takwini*) and can be acquired through studying the revelation (*tashri'i*).

Algazel operationalizes the positive traits:
Wisdom is a positive trait of the self which enables a

human being to freely and consciously distinguish positive from negative dispositions guided by reason (*takwini*) and revelation (*tashri'i*). It includes consciousness of self operating through free-will and conscience.

Courage is a positive trait by which the self regulates the "natural disposition of anger in defense to survive as an individual" through guidance from reason (*takwini*) and revelation (*tashri'i*).

Temperance is a positive trait by which the self regulates the "natural disposition to lust to survive as a species" through guidance from reason (*takwini*) and revelation (*tashri'i*).

Justice is a positive trait of the self in which the natural dispositions of anger in defense to survive as an individual and lust to survive as a species as well as cognition—seeing things as they really are—are kept in their proper place and given their due according to guidance from reason (*takwini*) and revelation (*tashri'i*). This is, the state of the mean or equilibrium of these three basic systems of the human being.

THE QURAN AND CENTERING THROUGH THE POSITIVE TRAITS

The Quran mentions these traits which bring about "centeredness" when they work together in balance and harmony giving equilibrium to the self. All four are referred to in one verse:

> " BELIEVERS ARE THOSE WHO BELIEVE IN GOD AND HIS MESSENGER, THEN THEY DOUBT NOT AND STRIVE (JIHAD) WITH THEIR BENEFITS (IN THE WAY OF GOD) AND STRIVE (JIHAD) WITH THEIR LIVES IN THE WAY OF GOD; THEY ARE THE TRUTHFUL ONES." (49:15)

*"Believers are those who believe in God and His Messenger
then they doubt not,"* a belief that is a consequence of reason
and consciousness as the highest form of wisdom, *"and
strive (jihad) with their benefits in the Way of God,"* indicating
temperance since this striving is only possible to be **in the
Way of God** (nature/nurture or *takwini/tashri'i* guidance)
when the unconscious, affective/emotive function is regulated by the rational, conscious belief in God and His Messenger,*"and strive with their lives in the Way of God,"* clearly
referring to the behavioral function and courage since this
positive trait is only possible of attainment **in the Way of
God** when the preconscious, behavioral function is regulated by the rational, conscious belief in God and His Messenger; *"they are the truthful ones, "* the just.

Each of the three positive traits: courage, temperance,
and wisdom may develop as negative traits through an
overdevelopment, underdevelopment, or undevelopment
of one of the three functions of affect, behavior, or cognition (fig. 5). Thus, whereas the positive traits are three, the
negative are nine. [12]

CONCLUSION

Becoming a fair and just person, having the other three
traits—wisdom, courage, and temperance in balance—is
to be "centered." However, finding center is a difficult
task. Naraqi explains:

To find the real center, which en-
tails absolute moderation, is difficult
to attain. To remain at this center and
to preserve this balance is even more
difficult.[13]

TO FIND CENTER
AND STAY THERE
IS DIFFICULT.

The Prophet said,

Surah Hud has made an old man of
me because of the verse, *'Tread the
Straight Path as you have been command-
ed.'"* (11:112)[14]

"TREAD THE
STRAIGHT PATH..."
— 11:112 AND PROPHETIC
TRADITION

According to psychoethics, being centered in wisdom, courage, and temperance, does not, however, result in being a just person. According to this psychological system, even if a person struggles with the self and becomes centered in the positive traits of wisdom, courage, and temperance, becoming what he feels to be is a just person, such a person has still not perfected his "self" in the **Way of God** unless these positive traits benefit other people also for the journey we are exploring towards centeredness depends on the self's relation to God, others, as well as self. If only the relationship of self to self were involved in centering, cognition would be sufficient in the Western view and there would be no need for actions. So the final condition of being centered is when others benefit from a person's striving towards perfecting nature in its mode of operation and if this not be real, there is no "centering." Dawwani says:

PROOF OF BEING CENTERED IS FOUND WHEN ANOTHER BENEFITS FROM THE CENTEREDNESS

Further, it is to be observed that until each of these positive traits operates on another person, the possessor of it is not entitled to praise. One centered with the positive trait of temperance is not called liberal unless another human being benefits from his liberalness. A person who considers himself centered on courage and the avoidance of harm/pain instinct is called irritable instead of courageous. A person who possesses intellectual cultivation is called clever instead of wise if another does not benefit from his wisdom.[15]

Therefore, one gages one's centeredness from the response of others. Dawwani goes on to say:

As soon as he produces an affect on others, whether he excites hope or fear of God, reverence and respect take root in their hearts. Then it becomes obligatory on their part to give him praise.

Throughout this journey, when we say one is entitled to praise, he has caused another person to want to praise him. Now it is clear that without people feeling hope in God or fear of God, they will never decide to give praise. No matter how perfected one's nature be, as long as others are neither attracted to his positive traits nor avoid by their own negative ones, no praise will be elicited. However, as soon as either case exists—attraction to the positive or avoidance of the negative—it becomes worthwhile, even obligatory upon those effected to ask how he developed. Happy is he who can thus help his fellow human being.[16]

> **STAGES:**
> HAVING SOUGHT
> **DIVINE ASSISTANCE**
>
> 1ST: CENTER SELF
>
> 2ND: BENEFIT ANOTHER
>
> 3RD: DESERVING PRAISE, RESPOND TO OTHERS ASKING TO LEARN
>
> 4TH CENTERED SELF PRACTICES COUNSELING TO POSITIVE TRAITS AND PREVENTING NEGATIVE ONES

Dawwani here points out that there are actually four stages involved. The first stage is to center the self. The second is for another to benefit from that centering as proof that it has actually occurred. The third stage is to have such an effect on another that they freely choose to move towards centering themselves. The fourth stage is the centered person practicing the religious obligation of counseling to positive traits and preventing the development of negative ones. The obligation implies responsibility and commitment to others. However, the obligation does not even arise towards others until a person has not

first taken responsiblity for self and committed self towards completing the first phase of perfection of nature in
its mode of operation, that of becoming centered. It is then
that the cycle begins and the self cannot consider itself
centered until another person has benefitted from that centeredness which then causes others to seek out centeredness and the centered person becomes responsible and
committed to them.

NOTES TO TOPOGRAPHY

1 Naraqi, p. 12.

2 Tusi, p. 39.

3 Rhazes, p. 39. For Rhazes, see Glossary.

4 See *Jihad Phase I.: Traditional Guidance and Centering the Self.*

5 *Ibid.*

6 Naraqi, p. 56.

7 *Ibid.*, p. 52.

8 *Ibid.*, p. 63.

9 *Ibid.*, p. 64.

10 See *Jihad Phase I: Traditional Guidance and Centering the Self.*

11 Algazel, *Tahafut*, p. 303.

12 See *Jihad Phase I: Traditional Guidance and Centering the Self* for a complete description of each of these subcategories of each positive trait, as well. Some aspects of the diagram on page vi can be found in the Enneagram or nine personality points. The nine personality points are considered to have been part of the oral tradition of the Naqshbandi Sufis in Central Asia which was imparted to Gurdjieff who then took it to Europe. It is also said to have been given to Oscar Ichazo who held workshops on it first in Chile and then in New York city. At the present time it is being used as a way to better understand the self particularly in Catholic pastoral counseling. Further description of the present diagram can be found in *Jihad Phase I: Traditional Guidance and Centering the Self*. Also, see Tusi in Glossary for a discussion of the three negative categories.

13 Naraqi, p. 70.

14 *Ibid.*, p. 70.

15 Dawwani, p. 54. For Dawwani, see Glossary.

16 *Ibid.*, pp. 66-67.

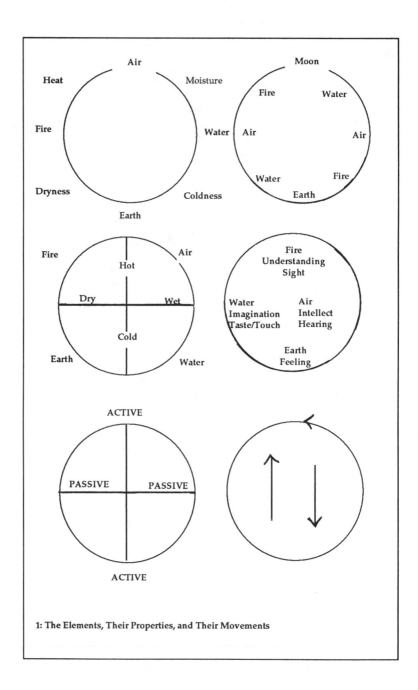

1: The Elements, Their Properties, and Their Movements

3
STRUCTURE

INTRODUCTION

The self is generated out of the Divine Spirit and natural dispositions of the mineral, plant, and animal forms, which are part of *takwini* guidance. It then may evolve the ability of consciousness through *tashri'i* guidance. This enhances the actualization of conscience and free-will as the self's own special natural disposition.

NATURAL DISPOSITION OF MINERALS

The elements, in the traditional perspective, develop in the atmosphere between the moon and the earth (fig. 1). Once on earth, they are preserved in the mineral "soul" or nature in its mode of operation as the Will of God. The elements are earth, air, fire, and water. Earth is dry and cold, water is cold and moist, air is hot and moist, and fire is hot and dry. Earth is the opposite of air and water is the opposite of fire. Union is possible because water acts as an intermediary between earth and air and air acts as an intermediary between water and fire.

The elements possess the natural disposition to ascend,

descend, and to move in a circular direction. Each element is joined by one of its qualities to that which is below it and above it—water to earth below it by coldness and water to air above by moisture; air to water below it by moisture and to fire above it by heat; fire to air below it by heat and to earth, towards which it inclines in a circular motion, by dryness; earth to water above it by coldness and to fire, which declines towards it, by dryness. The elements are continually produced one from the other and their energy is never lost. The movement of the elements produce the humors[1] within which, in turn, one's natural temperament is determined.

Two other functions these qualities have is that of being active or passive. Heat and cold are active while moisture and dryness are passive. Heat and cold are considered active because sometimes they draw on moisture and sometimes on dryness. A correspondence also exists between fire and understanding, air and reason, water and imagination and earth and the external senses where the four qualities are again repeated: fire is likened to sight, air to hearing, water to taste and smell and earth to feeling.

Natural Dispositions of Plants

Avicenna (d. 1037) explains what the plant or vegetive soul is and how it functions in the traditional perspective:

Vegetal State

When the elements are mixed together in a more harmonious way, i.e. in a more balanced proportion than in the [case of mineral forms] other beings also come into existence out of them due to the powers of the heavenly bodies. The first of these are plants. Now some plants are grown from seed and set aside a part of the

body bearing the reproductive function, while others grow from sponta-
neous generation without seeds. Since
plants nourish themselves they have
the function of nutrition. And because
it is of the nature of plants to grow, it
follows that they have the function of
growth. Again, since it is the nature of
certain plants to reproduce their like
and to be reproduced by their like,
they have a reproductive faculty. The
reproductive faculty is different from
the nutritive system, for unripe fruits
possess the nutritive but not the reproductive system; just as they possess the
faculty of growth, but not that of reproduction. Similarly, the nutritive
system differs from that of growth. Do
you not see that decrepit animals have
the nutritive system but lack that of
growth?

The nutritive system transmits food
and replaces what has been dissolved
with it; the growth system increases
the substance of the main structural organs in length, breadth, and depth, not
haphazard but in such a way that they
can reach the utmost perfection of
growth. The reproductive system gives
the matter the form of the thing; it separates from the parent body a part in
which a system derived from its origin
inheres and which, when the matter
and the place which are prepared to receive its activity are present, performs
its function.[2]

NUTRITIVE

ATTRACTION
RETENTION
REPULSION
DIGESTION

GROWTH

BREADTH
LENGTH
DEPTH

REPRODUCTION

ASEXUAL
BISEXUAL

NATURAL DISPOSITIONS OF ANIMALS/SELF

Animals inherit the natural dispositions of the mineral

and plant soul as nature in its mode of operation and two special natural dispositions of their own, namely, voluntary motivation and perception by organs.

ANIMALS' PERCEPTION BY ORGANS

With the evolutionary development of the animal, perception begins to operate to distinguish images from objects in reality. Perception as a function of the animal consists of five external and internal sensible and psychic senses. Avicenna first explains the external senses which are capable of a degree of knowledge and of pleasure and pain:

EXTERNAL SENSES

The external senses are each capable of a basic perception of things that are actually present to the external sense organs. Their perception, however, is based on a single kind of impression.

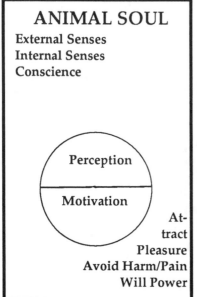

ANIMAL SOUL
External Senses
Internal Senses
Conscience

Perception

Motivation

Attract
Pleasure
Avoid Harm/Pain
Will Power

The perceptive faculty can be divided into two parts, the five external and the five internal senses.

One of the external senses is sight. It perceives the image of the forms of colored bodies imprinted on the vitreous humor. These forms are transmitted through actually transparent media to polished surfaces.

The second is the sense of hearing. It perceives the form of what is transmitted to it by the vibration of the air which is compressed between two objects, one striking and the other being struck, the latter offering it resistance so as to set up vibrations in the air which produce the sound. This vibration of the air outside reaches the air which lies motionless and compressed in the cavity of the ear, moving it in a way similar to that in which it is itself moved. Its waves touch that nerve and so it is heard.

The third sense is of that of smell. It perceives the odor conveyed to it by inhaled air, which is either mixed with the vapor in the air or is imprinted on it through qualitative change in the air produced by an odorous body.

The fourth sense is that of taste located in the nerves distributed over the tongue. It perceives the taste dissolved from bodies touching it and mingling with the saliva it contains, thus producing a qualitative change in the tongue itself.

The fifth sense is that of touch which is distributed over the entire skin and flesh of the body. The nerves perceive what touches them and are affected when it is opposed to them in quality and changes are then made in their constitution or structure. Probably this sense is not one species but a genus including four qualities which are distributed throughout the skin. The first of them judges the opposition between hot and cold; the second that between dry and moist; the third that between hard and soft; and the fourth that between rough and smooth. But their coexistence in the same organ gives the false impression that they are essentially one. The forms of all the sensibles reach the organs of sense and are imprinted on them, and then sensation perceives them. 3

THE
FIVE
EXTERNAL
SENSES

SIGHT

HEARING

SMELL

TASTE

TOUCH

TOUCH
DISTINGUISHES
COLD AND HOT
DRY AND MOIST
HARD AND SOFT
ROUGH AND SMOOTH

Avicenna is as explicit in regard to the description of the internal senses, as well.

INTERNAL SENSES

DATA FROM THE FIVE SENSES IS COLLECTED BY THE COMMON SENSE FUNCTION AND RETAINED IN REPRESENTATION.

INTERNAL SENSES
PERCEIVE IMPRESSIONS

PERCEIVE INTENTIONS

PERCEIVE AND ACT

PERCEIVE AND DO NOT ACT

PRIMARY PERCEPTION

SECONDARY PERCEPTION

There are some aspects of internal perception which perceive the form of the sensed things, and others which perceive the 'intention' thereof. Some faculties, again, can both perceive and act while others only perceive and do not act. Some possess primary perception, others secondary perception. The distinction between the perception of the form and that of the intention is that the form is what is perceived both by the inner self and the external sense; but the external sense perceives it first and then transmits it to the self, as, for example, when the sheep perceives the form of the wolf, i.e. its shape, form, and color. This form is certainly perceived by the inner senses of the sheep, but it is first perceived by its external sense. As for the intention, it is a thing which is perceived from the sensed object without its previously having been perceived by the external sense, just as the sheep perceives the intention of harm in the wolf, which causes it to fear the wolf and to flee from it, without harm having been perceived by the external senses. Now what is first perceived by the sense organs and then by the internal senses is the form, while the internal senses perceive intention without the external senses.

The distinction between perception accompanied or unaccompanied by action is this: it is the function of certain internal senses to combine certain perceived forms and intentions with others and to separate some of them from others, so that they perceive and also act on what they have perceived. Perception unaccompanied by action takes place when the form or the intention is merely imprinted on the sense organ without the percipient having any power to act upon it at all.

The distinction between primary and secondary perception is that in the form, the percipient faculty somehow directly acquires the form, while in the latter, the form is acquired through another agent which transmits it to the percipient faculty.[4]

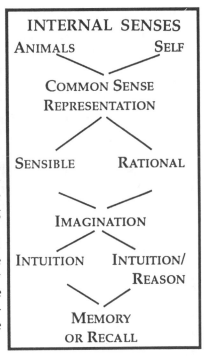

INTERNAL SENSES

ANIMALS   SELF

COMMON SENSE
REPRESENTATION

SENSIBLE   RATIONAL

IMAGINATION

INTUITION   INTUITION/
                       REASON

MEMORY
OR RECALL

Common sense, the first internal sense, is the storehouse for all impressions from the outer world. It directly receives the contents of the five external senses. For instance, when an apple is perceived, through the "common" sense, the self distinguishes the different states of the apple and realizes that every part of the apple possesses taste, smell, color, warmth, or cold.

There are four functions connected to common sense: to receive an impression; to act on it as arbiter of reports from the five external senses; to transmit the results to a more inward sense; to reduce contrary images to a unity of perception thereby destroying false impressions which may arise from several impressions received at the same time from different senses. It is the most basic sense of internal perception. Second is the internal sense of retaining forms or representation. This comes into action after common sense has stopped. It stores and retains the forms received by common sense.Third is sensible imagination in animals according to Avicenna:

SENSIBLE IMAGINATION

RECEIVES AND RETAINS ONLY SENSORY IMPRESSIONS

REARRANGES IMPRESSIONS WITH ADDITION AND SUBSTRACTION

ADDS OWN IMPRESSIONS

INTUITION

REDUCES IMPRESSIONS TO THEIR INTRINSIC INTENTION TO FORM A JUDGMENT

ADDS OWN INTENTIONS

Sensible imagination functions spontaneously or in subservience to intuition [the next internal sense]. Whether the perception functions collectively or singly, it receives and retains only sensory impressions. It rearranges the impressions with some addition and subtraction. Hence sensible imagination not only produces images derived from perception, but may occasionally add some of its own which may be contrary to all common sense. Retaining of forms, on the other hand, presents only those images which had been received earlier from common sense.

A fourth internal sense is intuition. It reduces perceived things to their intangible, intrinsic meanings to form a judgment which cannot be perceived by the senses either because the nature of the object does not show it or the object is not present at the time of judgment. Intuition is the process which informs the animals that a wolf is their enemy and that they have to take care of their young ones and that the shepherd is a friend who need not be shunned. It is obvious that love and hate are matters not of the external senses. Even though they may not be externally perceived but rather internally sensed by animals, there must be a separate process dictating such actions. Intuition differs from imagination in that the latter keeps the precepts as they are, while intuition adds a meaning to it which had not been communicated by any sense organ. Intuition gives a conative effect to that which has no perceptual basis. Just as common sense controls the sensory impressions, intuition directs the supersenuous ideas which are independent of common sense.

Memory [and/or recall] are the fifth internal sense. They are a store house for naturally disposed ideas but not for the precepts held by the retaining of forms function. [5]

MEMORY AND/OR RECALL
STORES NATURALLY DISPOSED IDEAS
DOES NOT INTERFERE IN STORAGE OF IMPRESSIONS WHICH REPRESENTATION HANDLES

SELF'S PERCEPTION FUNCTIONS

Perception is of three types: sensible, psychic, and cognitive/rational. The sensible functions include external and internal senses. Psychic and cognitive perception can be processed, as well, through the internal senses alone.

SENSIBLE PERCEPTION
EXTERNAL SENSES

The self has access to the same five external senses that an animal is capable of having and they operate through the same processes.

INTERNAL SENSES

Although common sense, representation, and sensible imagination are held in common by animals and the self, there are differences because of the human capacity for rationality.

Representation receives images that have been received and sorted by the common sense. Its main function within the self is to continue the thought process, to recommend important forms to the deliberations of rational imagination and to store them in memory. It retains impressions longer than the common sense does and tries them in balance.

PSYCHIC PERCEPTION
IMAGINATION

While being referred to as sensible imagination in animals, imagination forms the basis of psychical perception. Whereas sensible perception is particular, imagination is general and it culminates in cognitive or rational perception so that it is the intermediary between the sensible and the rational. It is active while the self is both awake and asleep and is the cause of dreams. It can operate out of either the immediate experience of intuition or out of the deliberations of reason.

Avempace (d. 1138) describes the internal sense of imagination and its relation to the rational system:

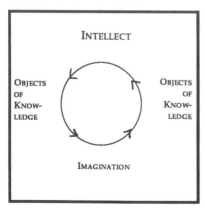

Look into the wonders that lie between the intellect and imagination through your penetrative soul. You can see with certainty that the intellect derives the objects of knowledge called the intelligibles from the imaginative sense and offers to the imaginative sense a number of other objects of knowledge. Take, for example, the moral and artistic ideals, or those objects of knowledge which are either the events that might take place and are available in the imaginative sense before their occurrence or the events that have not occurred but have found their way into the imaginative sense not through the sense-organs but rather through the intellect as in the case of true dreams. The most astonishing thing concerning the imaginative sense is that which relates to revelation. It is clear in these cases that what the intellect offers to the human imagination does not proceed from reason itself, nor is acted upon by reason, but arises in imagination through an agent who has known it beforehand, and is able to create it. It is God Who causes by His Will the mover of the active spheres to act upon the passive spheres as He likes. When, for example, He intends to make manifest what will occur in the universe, He first of all sends the knowledge to angels and through them to the human intellect. This knowledge comes to the human being in accordance with his capacity for receiving it. This is evident in most cases of God's virtuous servants Whom He has shown the right path and who are sincere to Him, particularly the Prophets to whom He makes manifest through His angels in waking life or dream the wonderful events that are going to happen in the universe.

God, the Almighty, makes manifest to His existing beings and creatures through both knowledge and deed. Every being receives these from

TRUE DREAMS

MORAL AND ARTISTIC IDEALS OR OBJECTS OF KNOWLEDGE WHICH ARE EITHER THE EVENTS THAT MIGHT TAKE PLACE— AND ARE AVAILABLE IN THE IMAGINATIVE SENSE BEFORE THEIR OCCURRENCE— OR EVENTS THAT HAVE NOT OCCURRED BUT APPEAR IN THE IMAGINATION— NOT THROUGH THE SENSE ORGANS BUT THROUGH THE INTELLECT.

EVERY CELESTIAL
BODY
POSSESSES INTELLECT
AND
NATURE IN ITS MODE
OF OPERATION
THROUGH WHICH
IT PERFORMS
PARTICULAR ACTIONS
WHICH ARE PER-
CEIVED BY
WAY OF IMAGINATION
OF
TRANSFERENCE FROM
AN IMAGINARY PLACE
WHICH CONTINUES
TO EXIST

Him according to its rank in the perfection of nature in its mode of operation: the intellects receive from Him knowledge according to their positions and spheres receive from Him figures and physical forms according to their ranks and positions. Every celestial body possesses intellect and nature in its mode of operation through which it performs particular actions which are perceived by way of imagination such as the imagination of transference from an imaginary place which continues to exist. Due to the individually perceptible particular transference there arise particular actions which are perceived by the bodies that come into being and pass away. This is most manifest in the sun and the moon from among the celestial bodies. It is through this intellect that a person knows sciences which are revealed to him from God, things that are intelligible, the particular events which are to take place in the present and the future, as well as the events that happened in the past. This is the knowledge of the unseen of which God informs His chosen servants through His angels.[6]

Avempace also says that there are various grades of knowledge, the first of which is knowledge of a specific, particular object. This comes into being by the apprehension of the particular in the imaginative sense. This is the weakest type of knowledge of an object and resembles the imagination of an animal. When, on the other hand, the state of the particular is possible in the imaginative sense, the self advances to this particular with its detailed characteristics which help it to recognize it to be the same at different times. It distinguishes John to be, for example, tall, dark, and handsome and considers all of these qualities to be related numerically to one individual. Avempace says that some people think that words introduce multiplicity where there is only unity as with tall, dark, and handsome to describe John. But, Avempace adds, this is the way the self achieves the knowledge of individual objects in so far as they are definite and particular.

When the imaginative sense obtains objects of imagination, the internal rational sense [to be discussed next], looks at them through its insight and realizes the universal meanings. Through these universal meanings, the rational sense imagines and distinguishes the nature of every imagined object. When the words indicating the universal meanings are referred to, the rational sense distinguishes them, presents them to reason, and apprehends them. This can happen in two basic ways: the rational sense presents the universal meanings to reason and apprehends them as true of the imagined objects or individuals signified by them. Through insight the rational sense sees the universal meanings. The rational sense then distinguishes universal meanings from them as described above.

The second basic way of interaction between imagination and the rational sense is when the rational sense distinguishes these universal meanings perfectly but when it sees them through its insight and presents them to the self in a well ordered manner, it sees them through its insight in the imaginative sense which also acts upon them and makes them resemble the universal meaning. It gives to them forms which are common to more than one, but not to all objects to which this meaning is applicable.

Avempace gives the example of a sculptor who represents the form of a horse in stone or a painter who draws

the form of a horse on a canvas. This representation is imperfect because it represents and reproduces the form of a
horse that is full grown. The drawing is not common to all
horses. The imaginative sense represents things which are
limited in respect of age, size, and so forth. The image of a
horse does not represent the full-grown horse, the young
horse, and the colt. Its image is common only to the horses
of that particular size or age which the imaginative sense
represents.

As soon as the rational sense makes distinctions of universal meanings and presents them to reason to look more
closely into them through its insight, the rational sense
looks at them through the image which the imaginative
sense represents. The rational sense distinguishes whether
the image is perfect or not perfect, common or not common. It thinks immediately of the intelligible meanings.
This is the way that universal meanings are understood by
artists and scientists. When the artist, for example, thinks
about how to make an object, he presents the image of the
particular article to his imagination and prepares his plan
to make it. Similarly, when a scientist looks into the object
of knowledge to know its nature and gives its description,
he presents its image to his imagination. Avempace adds
that whoever exerts the rational sense to act on the objects
obtained in the imagination, sees the confirmation of the
above description of process. This, he says, is like a person
who sees the light of the sun through the light of the sun
with the external sense of sight. This ability is a gift which
is like the light of the sun through which the self realizes
and sees the creation of God so clearly that the self becomes a believer in Him, His angels, Books, Prophets, and
the next world. It is this self that enjoys certain belief and
remembers God while standing, sitting, and lying down.
Every thought is obtained through this gift which is no

other than the self's connection with the Active Intellect.

Imagination writes in memory impressions of things received by the five external senses as well as by reason in addition to things it composes itself. It is like a person who writes himself a note to remind himself of something and later reads the note and mentally adds something from his mind at that moment to the note. Later imagination may return to the forms and activate them without the intervention of the external senses. In this case, it is activated by the affective or behavioral systems attracting the self to pleasure or avoiding harm from the self. It has also been noted that imagination is more likely to follow the sense than reason. Once the senses are satiated, imagination is freed to busy itself with other forms. Imagination is never idle. It often leads the self to confusion.

It is quite possible for imagination to oppose reason. Since it is closer to the external senses than it is to reason, it may allure the self to the affective or behavioral systems to establish a coalition against reason. Rash judgments are strengthened in this way.

Imagination plays a crucial role in the self. It evolves ideals and is naturally disposed to pass those that are of sufficient magnitude onto reason for deliberation. It also communicates with the heart where the energy of the affective-behavioral systems resides. It has to do with both thought and action. It receives sense impressions before the self can respond. Imagination has considerable authority in the self. Because of its freedom and its dual relation to reason and the affective-behavioral systems, it exercises an important influence on conduct which may not be to the best advantage of the self in its process of centering as it is considered that right conduct comes from reason.

COGNITIVE/RATIONAL PERCEPTION

The fourth internal sense marks cognitive or rational perception within the self. Cognition may be achieved in two basic ways: first through discursive reasoning, deliberation, and drawing conclusions. This is referred to as reason or rationality. The second type of cognition is that of direct awareness or experience and is referred to as intuition. With the latter, cognition is attained without learning or making an effort to acquire cognition. The first type forms the basis for the process of centering in Phase I of the Greater Jihad. According to Farabi (d. 950) intuition is the most noble level of self-apprehension where the hidden is unveiled. It is the level of communion, ecstasy, and inspiration and it forms the basis for Phase II of the Greater Jihad. [7]

INTUITION AND/OR REASON

Making up the fourth internal sense, intuition/reason can operate without any sensible impressions. As reason, this type of internal perception is inclined towards the deduction of sciences, crafts, and the perception of intelligibles. Just as sensible imagination contained the ability to perceive information from the external senses and motivate attraction to pleasure and avoidance of harm, so, also, reason has a perceptive ability and a motivational one. Its perceptive ability is that of deliberation and understanding. Its motivating force is that of free-will.

These two—reason and free-will—are referred to as the practical intellect. As the final point on action, the practical intellect receives and illuminates ideas that have come from imagination. It also has a reflective power by which it examines its own actions and certain innate criteria which provide knowledge of takwini and tashri'i guidance. Because of these natural dispositions, the self not only comprehends particular forms, but is also able to distinguish between positive and negative dispositions and ultimately to arrive at Divine Truth.

These functions are performed without using instruments of the body. Reason or understanding perform different functions and for each receives different names. These are sub-categories of wisdom that continue the work begin by imagination: reason, discourse, penetration or sagacity, judgment, understanding, will. The latter is the consequence of the knowing process by which the mind reaches out for the positive.

Reason is used when the intellect considers material things and understanding is used by which universal, spiritual truths are comprehended. When reason strives towards contemplation, it is called the cognitive intellect. When it seeks the positive and having found it goes forward to the will in order that the self may follow the positive or flee from the negative, it is called the practical intellect which contains the Active Intellect within itself. It is also referred to as prudence. From each of the functions a habit of life may develop—contemplative or active. The word active is used in regard to the practical intellect because it does not stop with the discovery of a positive or negative trait but goes forward with the will.

MEMORY AND/OR RECALL

The fifth sense is that of memory or recall. Natural dispositions are held in storage here which the self only needs to be reminded of to recall. It does not, however, hold the forms gathered by common sense and retained by the second internal sense.

ANIMALS' MOTIVATION

In addition to perception, the animal also contains the

motivational system as part of the animal soul. Motivation, including will power, renders the animal capable of action. Motivation is of two types: the first gives an impulse requiring a voluntary response and the second involuntarily causes the body to react on its own accord. When a pleasurable or painful image is imprinted on the internal sense called sensible imagination in the animal, it rouses it to movement. This impulsive arousal has two subdivisions. Avicenna explains:

ATTRACT TO PLEASURE AVOID HARM/PAIN

... one is called 'the pleasure principle' or lust which provokes a movement (of the organs) that brings one near to things imagined to be necessary or useful in the search for pleasure. The second is called 'the pain principle' or anger, which impels the subject to a movement of the limbs in order to avoid things imagined to be harmful or destructive, and thus to overcome them.[8]

As previously stated, these two naturally disposed, unconscious/ preconscious functions within the animal make-up the two basic systems of animal forms. Known in philosophy as the concupiscible or attraction to benefit and irascible or repulsion of harm faculties, in psychological terms they are referred to as "attraction to pleasure" or "the pleasure principle" and "avoidance of pain" or "the pain principle." They are essentially the unconscious, affective/emotive and the preconscious, behavioral systems.

SELF'S VOLUNTARY MOTIVATION

The self's voluntary motivation contains, in addition to the properties of animal motivation, free-will. It is the highest form of motivation in nature's mode of operation and is independent of conscience or reason. It may do as it pleases, but the self will be held responsible on the Day of Judgment for the decisions that it makes.

ANIMALS' COMBINED PERCEPTION/MOTIVATION

Animals have functions that combine perception and motivation. They are considered to have the beginnings of the practical intellect in the sense of motivation to action and a sense of right and wrong which they are obliged to obey without question.

SELF'S COMBINED PERCEPTION/MOTIVATION

The self shares the above two impulsive systems of attraction to pleasure and avoidance of pain with animals and, in addition, has a third which is the cognitive system, combining aspects from both perception and motivation.

THE SELF'S COGNITIVE SYSTEM

The cognitive system is the control center for thought and actions of the self's conscience, free-will, and ability to gain consciousness of self. The norm in psychoethics is for the cognitive system to regulate the preconscious (not to the extent that it can come to know, but to the extent that it can be disciplined) behavioral and unconscious affective natural dispositions by keeping them in a state of equilibrium or moderation in terms of the Straight Path. We again turn to Avicenna for a description of the cognitive system within the self:

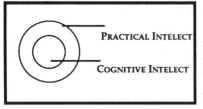

The cognitive [human rational/ consciousness] system of self is divisible into a practical and a cognitive function, both of which are equivocally called the intellect). [9]

The cognitive system contains the practical intellect which, in turn, contains the cognitive intellect. It is through the cognitive intellect that the self understands things that it cannot bring into being and it is through the practical intellect that the self understands and brings them into being in accordance with its own intention. The description of the cognitive system begins with the practical intellect because its role is far more significant in the centering process than the cognitive intellect. As Averroes (b. 1126) explains, the seat of human creativity is the practical intellect.[10]

THE INTELLECT
Practical Intellect

The self is equipped through *takwini* guidance with what is known as the practical intellect as part of the process of nature in its mode of operation. According to Avempace, objects are created through the organs of the human body either by the movement of the organs without any tool from the outside or by moving the organs which in turn move some external instrument. Human organs are motivated to move but when something is created, it is first created by free-will in the mind and then it is produced outside the mind in accord with the image formed in the mind before the organs produce it. The first image disappears from the self and another replaces it and the process continues.

Whenever the self intends to create something, it first forms an image of it in the practical intellect which transfers it to the internal sense of imagination. The self then sets the organs into motion to bring it into being. The practical intellect understands and abstracts in imagination.

When the practical intellect operates out of the internal sense of imagination, it abstracts the image of the thing to be created according to a particular form or size. Self-motivation then moves the organs to create the object. Thus it is the practical intellect which first creates the thing and not self-motivation of the organs. The self is naturally disposed to motivation but only does so in the Creative Act when the practical intellect causes the thing to be created to appear in the internal sense of imagination. Only after that does self-motivation cause the things to be created by the use of the organs.

The practical intellect, then, has two functions according to Avempace: to present to the internal sense of imagination the image of the thing to be created; and to have the thing come into being outside the self by motivating the organs of the body.[11]

Avicenna explains the functions of the practical intellect.

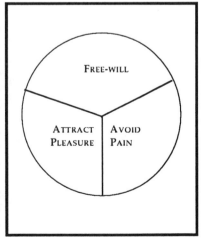

The practical function is the principle of movement of the human body which urges it to individual actions characterized by deliberation and in accordance with purposive considerations. This function has a certain correspondence with motivation [and with the internal perceptive senses of] imagination and reason, and a certain dual character in itself.

Its relationship to motivation is that certain states arise in it peculiar to the self by which it is disposed to quick ac-

PRACTIAL
INTELLECT

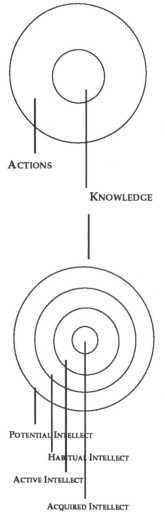

ACTIONS

KNOWLEDGE

POTENTIAL INTELLECT

HABITUAL INTELLECT

ACTIVE INTELLECT

ACQUIRED INTELLECT

tions and emotions such as shame, laughter, weeping, and so forth. Its relationship to the internal senses of imagination and reason is that it uses those senses to deduce plans concerning transitory things and to deduce human arts.

Finally, its own dual character is that with the help of the cognitive intellect, it forms the ordinary and commonly accepted opinions concerning actions, as, for instance, that lies and tyranny are negative traits and other similar premises which differ from purely rational actions. This function must regulate all the other functions of the body lest negative traits control the self and not allow the self to perfect its nature through the actualization of positive traits.

If we examine them more closely, the reason why positive traits are attributed to this cognitive system is that the self is a single substance which is related to two planes—the one higher and the other lower than itself. It has special functions which establish the relationship between itself and each plane: the practical function which the self possesses in relation to the lower plane, which is the body, is its control and management; and the cognitive function in relation to the higher plane, from which it passively receives and acquires ideas. It is as if our self has two faces: one turned towards the body, and it must not be dominated by any requirements of the physical nature, and the other turned towards the higher principles, and it must always be ready to receive from what is there in the higher plane and to be influenced by it. [12]

According to Averroes it is through the practical intellect that the self loves or hates, lives in society, and has friends and positive dispositions.[13] The practical intellect is the locus of the highest forms of perception and motivation. The highest form of nature in its mode of operation in the perceptive system within the self is the conscience which is the source of the general principles upon which morality is based. The highest form of nature in its mode of operation in the voluntary motivational system is choice or free-will. It receives sensible and cognitive stimuli from the external and internal senses. When the stimuli are purely sensible, they have been first passed from the senses to the attraction to pleasure or avoidance of harm systems and from there to the practical intellect where a response is given. When the stimuli are purely cognitive, they pass directly into the practical intellect for action. When the stimuli are both sensible and cognitive, the practical intellect is the locus of operation for deliberation and the production of some action including human arts and sciences. The practial intellect contains the cognitive intellect and the latter develops through four stages.

THE COGNITIVE INTELLECT

There are four stages in the acquiring of the cognitive intellect which is held in preparedness within the practical intellect. Each one is called an intellect. Once the practical intellect acquires these intellects by completing the perfection of nature in its mode of operation within the self, that is, when the self is centered, the practical intellect then operates through the Active Intellect. The four stages are: potential, habitual, Active, and acquired intellects.

At the first stage of the potential intellect, the self thinks nothing but is prepared to think. Here the intellect cannot be creative in the act of knowledge. It is simply receptive to it. If there is actual knowledge at this stage, the self will not understand the reality of it. Out of this, through "reminders" grows the habitual intellect. Here the possibility of actualizing the potential intellect's preparedness exists. This means knowing the principles or axioms of knowledge like the whole is greater than the sum of its parts. The Active Intellect is the stage when the self no longer needs matter. It is solely concerned with intellectual demonstrations and is either acquired or bestowed as a Divine Gift. The Active Intellect, the center of all forms of thought, has a natural disposition by which it can reflect and then perform the act of thinking. It also has a reflective power by which it examines its own actions and certain criteria of its natural disposition which provides a knowledge of the law of God and nature. By virtue of these naturally disposed notions, the self not only comprehends particular and material forms, but, also, as a result of several processes, distinguishes between positive and negative traits and arrives ultimately at universal and Divine truths. The Active Intellect operates through three stages: exercise of deliberation; exercise of conscience; drawing conclusions.

Finally there is the acquired intellect which is the highest stage of the intellects. These stages are like signs upon the way of centering of self and beyond. The traveler is always the self. At the stage of the acquired intellect, "every conceptual form potentially contained in the self becomes apparent to it, like the face of a person reflected in a mirror held before him," according to Tusi.[14]

Here acquisition ceases. All the forms exist in the cognitive intellect, held within the practical intellect, which is in a state where the self can perform the act of thinking which occurs when the Active Intellect causes the habitual intellect to reflect back on itself and through this process, the self begins to think about the forms it has.

Averroes speaks of three basic operations of the cognitive intellect:

First we get in the intellect single notions (intentions) totally abstracted from matter. Secondly we combine two or more notions together to arrive at a concept. Then since concepts are neither true or false, we have to draw a conclusion.[15]

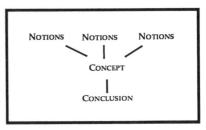

The cognitive intellect, then, is concerned with the cognition of truth. The objects that this natural disposition deals with are necessary, universal, and unchangeable like mathematical properties. They can be contemplated, but not deliberated for there is only one truth. The cognitive intellect is the part of the perceptive system where forms are imprinted. If the form exists in matter, it abstracts them. If they are already abstract, it receives them. It is located within the practical intellect.

THE PROCESS OF ACTIVATING THOUGHT/ACTION

The process of thought in which action results, according to psychoethics, can be described in the following way. When an object is perceived by the external senses (seeing, hearing, tasting, touching, smelling), nervous energy enables each organ effected to receive a particular kind of impression to which it has been naturally disposed to adapt. The impressions are sometimes vague and may be contradictory. Nervous energy hastens to the locus of the "common" sense where the impressions of the external senses are reduced to a unity and stored in the internal sense of representation which continues the thought process and gives the image to the internal sense of imagination.

This internal sense, having been able to elaborate ideas because of the nervous energy it has received, may assign the images to memory or may recommend them to reason and understanding before storing them for future use. If action is required, imagination communicates to the heart informing it about the pleasure or pain of the object. At the same instant, the images or ideas, compounded by the imagination from their original, simple impressions, are abstracted and perceived by reason. Reason deliberates and draws a conclusion which it presents to the free-will as positive or negative. Free-will, being the final decision maker, then decides to accept or reject the counsel of reason. The affective-behavioral systems obey free-will and set to work those things necessary for action. They command the self to motion to attract the pleasure or avoid pain.

This is the procedure for thought/action when the cognitive system is in balance. If the nurturing process has not been oriented towards preserving the healthy self, reason's advice will not be accepted by free-will. Free-will may even be bypassed by the affective-behavioral systems and respond to imagination themselves, singularly or together, in commanding the self to action.

The external-internal senses involved in sensible perception are naturally disposed to cooperate in such a way that each lower sense provides an image or stimulus adequate to the needs of the sense directly above it. Impressions received by the external senses become increasingly "abstracted" and "purified of the sensible," passing through the psychical perception of imagination until they culminate in the cognitive system's positive disposition of wisdom. Thus knowledge passes through several levels from the single sensible impression of each one of the external senses involved, through psychical perception, to the extent of spiritual truths. The self then understands many things which are beyond impressions provided by the external senses, from which the spirit of self is moved just as the external senses are moved by external objects.

The knowledge that we receive from the external senses is like shadows of them. The knowledge we have from common sense, representation, and imagination is as if we looked upon the images with more clarity than their shadows. The knowledge we have of understanding is as if we viewed not only the shadows and clear images of things, but also their very presence. The knowledge we have by reason is as if in addition to the shadow, clear image, and presence of an object, we saw its effects as well so that the nature of the object as it really is may be known.

Perception, then evolves ideas in various stages of completion. The degree of perception is accompanied by a corresponding degree of motivation. First is the perception of the external senses of which nervous energy present in organs give elementary knowledge of an object from which a stimulus comes. This perception is limited. For instance, if an object perceived is too large, sight needs the help of the internal senses. None of the external senses, without the help of imagination and memory, can build up impressions.

Next come psychical impressions in the imagination which have not external form or abstract images of understanding. Each of these may give rise to an attraction to pleasure or avoidance of pain response. From the imagination proceed the affective-behavioral systems of the heart. From understanding proceeds will.

CONCLUSION
The structure of the self develops out of nature in its

mode of operation in the mineral, plant, and animal. It shares the elements and their qualities with minerals; assimilative, reproductive, and growth functions with the plant; and perception and motivation with animals. The self begins to distinguish itself from the animal at the level of the third internal sense where it can employ free-will to obey God's Will while the animal has no choice but to obey God's Will.

Out of motivation comes the attraction to pleasure and avoidance of harm as well as free-will. Out of perception the self's conscience is illuminated. The practical intellect evolves out of the combination of perception and motivation. Out of the practical intellect, the cognitive intellect develops. When the practical intellect is served by conscience, free-will and understanding, it reflects on self through the presence of the Active Intellect and becomes conscious of self. The practical intellect, itself, is then called the Active Intellect. In order to be more certain that centering will be attained, Algazel says the natural way is for the Active Intellect to consciously exercise its free-will towards that which is more difficult. This way the self can be more assured that it is allowing the cognitive system to regulate. But even then, according to psychoethics, the only way to be sure of being centered is through receiving Divine Assistance.

The appearance of the Active Intellect marks the beginning of *Jihad Phase I: Traditional Guidance and Centering the Self*. Once centered, it is the Active Intellect operating out of the internal sense of imagination, bypassing reason and deliberation, now that they regulate the self, and moving as a spiraling center on the conscious return to the Source and this is *Jihad Phase II*.

NOTES TO STRUCTURE

1 An important separation developed in Islamic thought in regard to the role played by the humors. It would appear that traditional Western thought never separated physiology from psychology in the sense that unhealthy psychic states were seen to be caused by an imbalance in the natural disposition of one's temperament which comes from an imbalance in the humors. Traditional Muslim thought, however, very early on, separates physiology from psychology. Imbalances in temperament developing from imbalance in the humors means the need for medical attention through a diagnosis of the humors, part of the Natural Sciences. Imbalances in dispositions developing from imbalances in habits means the need for psychoethical treatment, part of Practical Philosophy, namely, the Science of Ethics. In the traditional Muslim perspective, then, what is temperament in medicine is disposition in psychoethics and what are the four humors in medicine, are the four positive traits of wisdom, temperance, courage, and justice in psychoethics.

2 Rahman, *Avicenna's Psychology*, p. 24.

3 *Ibid.*, pp. 26-27.

4 *Ibid.*, p. 30.

5 Avicenna (Ibn Sina), *Qanun*, p. 45. See Glossary.

6 Avempace (Ibn Bajjah), p. 571. See Glossary.

7 See *Jihad II: Spiraling on the Return*.

8 Rahman, *Avicenna's Psychology*, p. 26.

9 *Ibid.*, p. 32.

10 Averroes (Ibn Rushd), p. 552. See Glossary

11 *Ibid.*

12 Rahman, *Avicenna's Psychology*, pp. 32-33.

13 Averroes (Ibn Rushd), p. 553.

14 Tusi, p. 575.

15 Averroes (Ibn Rushd), p. 553.

DIVINE SPIRIT

MINERALS

HOT
COLD
MOISTURE DRYNESS

PLANTS

RETENTIVE/ASSIMILATIVE   EXCRETIVE
NUITRITIVE/DIGESTIVE
GROWTH
REPRODUCTIVE

ANIMALS

PERCEPTION   MOTIVATION

FIVE EXTERNAL SENSES   PRESERVE SPECIES/ INDIVIDUAL

FIVE INTERNAL SENSES   LUST AND ANGER

COMMON SENSE RECEIVES   OBEY AND IMPEL

RETAINING FORMS   ATTRACT PLEASURE/
                                            AVOID HARM

IMAGINATION

SENSIBLE   RATIONAL

INTUITION   REASON

MEMORY/RECALL

SELF

POTENTIAL INTELLECT
HABITUAL INTELLECT
ACTIVE INTELLECT
ACQUIRED INTELLECT

COGNITIVE INTELLECT

PRACTICAL INTELLECT

Structure of the Self

4
DYNAMICS

INTRODUCTION

The entire human organism is a complete system that makes use of energy transformed from food and air to satisfy its various natural dispositions. Dynamics works from perception to motivation and motivation to perception. Motivation is the seat of impulses towards inclinations which are imprinted on the external or internal senses and then, through filtering into the practical intellect, a response is given. Three energy sources are active in this perspective: natural (venial, *tabi'iya*), vital (arterial, *nafsaniyah*), and nervous (*hawaniyah*). These transformed energies are distributed throughout the body. The heart is considered to be the point of contact between the energy of the body and that of the self.

NATURAL ENERGIES OF THE LIVER

Energy in the liver undergoes successive processes of sublimation in the heart and brain. The purity of this energy and according to the function it performs as naturaly, vital, or nervous energy, serves a group of powers of nature in its mode of operation.

Vegetal functions promote nutrition, growth, and reproduction. The nutritive function works by a number of subordinate systems: retention, digestion, assimilation, expulsion. The energy for the vegetal functions originates in the liver where the humors are, as well. The humors move by natural energy through the veins carrying sustenance to the body, performing the tasks of the vegetal systems. A natural appetite, guided by nature in its mode of operation, instructs these various powers. Since the vegetal system cannot function separate from the body, it is mortal. It withers with age and when the body dies, neither the vegetal nor sensitive systems die but rather each stops functioning when its instruments, the parts of the body, fail.

VITAL ENERGY OF THE HEART

Natural energy of the vegetal functions arises from blood in the liver. It passes with the humors through the veins to all parts of the body. Some natural energy and humors enter the cavity of the heart and through transformation there, becomes the vital energy, a substance less gross than that of the liver. Vital energies are carried to the organs of the body by arteries. They make life possible. Vital energies are transformed in the brain where they become nervous energy. This makes perception and motivation to movement possible.

Vital energy of the sensitive functions arise from blood in the heart as transformed natural energy and move by way of the body through the arteries. The heart is the seat of life, of heat, of pulse, of the vital energies, and of nature in its mode of operation. It is the organ which lives first and dies last.

COGNITIVE VITAL AND NERVOUS ENERGIES RESPOND TO NATURAL DISPOSITIONS

A natural disposition of the self is activated as a cognitive representation of a physiological, affective, behavioral, or cognitive need. It is a desire to fulfill the natural dispositions of attracting the self to pleasure, avoiding harm/pain, and/or cognition which includes conscience, choice, and consciousness of self.

Nervous energy arises in the brain from the vital energy reaching it from the heart. The brain is the center for motivation and perception. Motivation allows movement and perception consists of external and internal senses.

The natural, physiological disposition of attraction to pleasure, mentally represented as a need, for instance, for food, causes the body to respond to a physiological need to preserve the individual. The natural, affective disposition, mentally represented as, for instance, grief, causes the body to respond to an affective need to preserve the individual. The natural, physiological disposition to avoid harm or pain, mentally represented as a need, for instance, to defend the self from harm, causes the body to respond to a physiological need. The natural, behavioral disposition to avoid harm or pain, mentally represented as a need, for instance, to show anger, causes the body to respond to a behavioral need.

COGNITIVE ENERGIES FOR CONSCIOUSNESS

The cognitive disposition of imagination, growing out of perception, may be represented as, for instance, an impression of "its time to eat" or "the self is endangered" or it may be to tell the hunger instinct "you just ate" or the defensive instinct "you are not in danger," regulating them and keeping them centered within the mean or a cognitive disposition itself such as "I will, therefore I am!"

AWAKENING THE NATURAL DISPOSITION TO CONSCIOUSNESS OF SELF

The natural cognitive disposition in the self is served by nervous energy. It has greater needs than that of other animals because of the human abilities to become conscious of self, conscious of the difference between positive and negative dispositions, and conscious of free-will. Consciousness is developed through "reminders" or Signs that remind the self of its origin and of the nobility it gained when it received the infusion of the Divine Spirit, signified by human values. They include the knowledge that God is One, that truth, beauty, goodness, and love exist and are expressed in the original creation which the self tries to imitate in response to a natural disposition to creativity, imitating the Original Creation.

Mutahhari (d. 1979) refers to the process to bring about consciousness in the traditional perspective. He refers to what is known in the West as the Socratic method. That is, the self becomes aware of the reality of self when reminded by some Sign without there being a need for reason. This is one of the methods used by the Quran.

The traditional perspective is that the self is created with a natural disposition towards following the natural Way of Life (*din*, religion) of nature in its mode of operation. The self at birth, however, knows nothing. *"And God brought you forth from the wombs of your mothers—you knew not anything and He gave you hearing and sight and hearts that you may give thanks."* (16:78) It only needs to be reminded to remember. Several times the Quran says to Muhammad (ﷺ), *"So you go on reminding; you are only a Reminder."* (88:21) Even one of the names of the Quran is "Reminder." (See 15:9)

This shows there is something in the self that requires no reasoning. A reminder of it is sufficient. The method used is that of the rhetorical question, whereby another Sign answers. It is a method which can help a person break through blockages in the mind caused by paradoxes and contradictions and this leads to consciousness of self. The Quran, as pointed out, uses this method when it says, *"What! Can those who know be equal to those who know not?"* (39:9) or *"Shall We treat those who believe and do good deeds like those who corrupt the earth? Or shall We treat the pious ones like the wicked ones?"* (38:28) and then answers in another verse, *"Only those possessed of intelligence will bear it in mind."* (13:19)

Arousing the Natural Disposition of Conscience

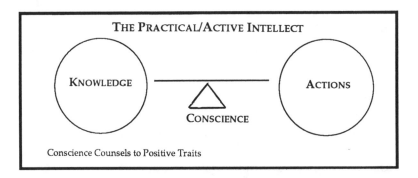

The practical intellect is the locus of operation of the conscience. It is a natural disposition of the self and exists in some form in animals who are naturally disposed to know that their very survival depends on them staying with the mean, on the Straight Path. The conscience of the self is also naturally predisposed but because of free-will, the self is free to accept or reject the advice of the conscience.

ACTIVATING THE NATURAL DISPOSITION TO FREE-WILL

Free-will is the highest evolutionary form of motivation in nature's mode of operation. It is naturally disposed by *takwini* guidance to be fair and just as well as to avoid conflict. This latter, avoiding conflict, is the stronger natural disposition. When the nurturing process is oriented towards preserving psychic health, free-will is gradually trained to accept the counsel of cognition. Cognition, as has been mentioned, contains both the cognitive and practical intellect.

Through habit, free-will has learned to seek the counsel of cognition before making a decision. The cognitive aspect of self has, through habit, learned to operate out of its most natural locus, the internal sense of reason. It deliberates, comes to an understanding of the situation, and draws a conclusion. Free-will is then free to accept or reject the conclusion. However, as free-will has a choice, it makes the final decision. The cognitive aspect of self is only a guide, a counselor. Free-will is naturally disposed to be higher than rationality.

If free-will accepts the advice, the self is regulated by the cognitive system in a state of balance and harmony, centered in the positive dispositions of temperance, courage, and wisdom. If another benefits from this centeredness, the self has attained the highest of the positive dispositions, that of being fair and just towards the Creator, the self, nature, and others.

FREE-WILL REBELS AGAINST REASON

When the nurturing process has not fostered the development of a healthy psychic self, the cognitive system has not been nurtured to operate out of reason. Instead, it operates out of the locus of intuition through imagination.

The process is explained like this: free-will seeks the

advice of reason. Reason responds through imagination, an internal sense, as has been shown, that is more firmly connected to the affective/behavioral systems than to the cognitive system. The irrational alliance of free-will and affect-behavior combine to force the cognitive system to develop numerous rationalizations and legitimations of desires of which the affective-behavioral systems could never conceive. The self develops what is called overconsciousness.

In this situation, instead of free-will exercising its natural disposition to fairness and justice, it falls under its stronger natural disposition to avoid conflict. In doing so, it loses its own liberty and freedom, allowing unconscious and preconscious forces to dominate. As the affect-behavior systems are not capable of consciousness, they are not able to regulate the self, but can only dominate it.

Free-will often refuses the advice of reason just to show that it is free. Everything depends on the decision of free-will. Reason is only a guide. Free-will, then, is subject to depravity which extends to all aspects of self. It may be depraved through false reasoning or through its own waywardness as unrestrained freedom and an inclination to content the senses. When free-will turns from understanding and reason, there is nothing the self can do but exercise its power in agreement with the external senses. To retrieve a perverted will is considered to be almost impossible.

FREE-WILL ALLIES WITH IMAGINATION AGAINST REASON

Imagination is likely to become an enemy of reason. As it is near the outer senses, it may seduce the self to accept some attachment and then, as an intermediary between the external senses and the affective-behavioral systems, establish a coalition against reason. This could explain how rash judgments are strengthened in imagination, arousing the affective-behavioral systems, and over-throwing reason. Imagination can be a dangerous guide to the self in terms of its centering process.

FREE-WILL ALLIES WITH IMAGINATION
AND THE EXTERNAL SENSES AGAINST REASON

Knowledge, it will be recalled, is dependent upon the external senses because they are the doors through which all impressions from the world pass to higher functions of thought and desire. Reason and imagination can only judge what they receive.

The senses may dominate reason. The ready response of reason to reports from the senses make of conscience a fleeting thing, yielding quickly to a new stimulus. Mention of words like judgment, reward, innocence, arrogance, all suffice to move conscience. The senses are easily moved by the affective-behavioral systems. A picture or mere description is enough to awaken passions of love or grief.

The strength of sense impressions as opposed to reason can be recalled when the self reflects on the parting of two friends. The idea of some particular gesture in a parting friend strikes us more deeply than all the reasoning in the world. The sound of a name repeated, certain words or a sad tone go to our very heart. A present object moves the affective-behavioral system much more vehemently than does perception through recall. In absence, the imagination represents the pleasure as far off and not prepared, but the thing being present, nothing seems to be left but to attain the desire. The desires of the affective-behavioral system become contagious through their outward manifestations. Inward functions respond quickly to sense impressions.

The external senses are capable of a degree of knowledge and of pleasure and pain. Since they cannot comprehend the full meaning of objects presented to them, they report to the self merely outward images and in their impressions emphasize qualities agreeable to sense rather than to the general welfare of the self. Not knowing all that takes place in imagination and in reason, they may accept enemies as friends. Through their strength, they may provoke serious disturbances in the self.

They work on imagination and without waiting for reason to deliberate, they alarm the affective-behavioral systems to the extent that the voice of reason cannot be heard nor the advice of understanding be accepted by free-will. Representing pleasures that are most apparent and present, they strongly provoke the affective system. Even though they are the self's first teacher, instead of freeing the self from deceit, they are seen to be able to deceive it themselves.

Free-will Allies with Imagination in the Affective-Behavioral Systems Against Reason

The affective-behavioral systems are naturally disposed to allow the self to regulate them through the cognitive system. When they join in an alliance with free-will, they follow the external senses. The senses respond to an object. Reason deliberates. Free-will is naturally disposed towards the positive as is reason. However, when under the influence of the affective-behavioral systems, free-will only sees the present which fills the imagination more readily than does the future and reason is subdued.

Free-will is a superior function to the affective-behavioral systems. It is joined with reason in the same way the affective-behavioral systems are joined to imagination. The self is naturally disposed to guide free-will towards action which is for the welfare of the self. However, the self contains an inferior kind of thought-action and that is of imagination and the affective-behavioral systems. Both of the latter act rashly without the deliberation of reason.

They are often too powerful to allow reason to advise and free-will to accept its advice.

The will is easily misled. Naturally inclined to avoid conflict, it succumbs to the affective-behavioral systems. They all grow out of motivation in the self and so have an established relationship. Reason can control action only through free-will and free-will frequently yields to the affective-behavioral systems. Strife in the self is most often between reason and the systems arising out of motivation. The external senses entice the imagination and it joins with the affective-behavioral systems and they, in turn, entice free-will away from following reason.

CENTERING THROUGH FREE-WILL

As nature in its mode of operation was perfected by the Creator in the self with the gift of consciousness, by-passing free-will causes an imbalance in the natural harmony and equilibrium of the self. This is because within the self, the process of free-will consciously seeking the counsel of reason is the regulator of nature in its mode of operation within the self. When the regulator is bypassed, the system loses its balance and equilibrium. If the nurturing process has not been able to preserve the healthy self, psychoethics provides the means to restore health.

If free-will accepts the guidance of reason, the self can become centered. The ideas upon which the reason deliberates come from the imagination. This sense may be functioning according to the Divine Will, operating through *takwini* and *tashri'i* guidance. This process becomes strong when good habits are formed in the self from birth.

Without this, the self becomes prone to negative traits and its free-will is not inclined towards choosing positive ones. It is motivated by its natural disposition of attraction to pleasure, the original goal of which is to preserve the species, but when it is unregulated, even the species is threatened by over, under or un-developed eating, sex, drinking, and so forth. The mirror of self is so encrusted with rust and dust that the self no longer has a vision of itself. It becomes alienated from its natural disposition and loses all sense of identity and direction. The self readily then forgets its original goal of submission to the Will of God by completing the perfection of nature in its mode of operation, that is, becoming conscious of self. It is no longer able to avoid pain/harm because the natural disposition of even its immunity systems break down. Free-will, naturally disposed to be free to choose to submit to the Will of God, is no longer free but enslaved by the self's affective and behavioral systems leading to the tyranny of the self in complete opposition to its original natural disposition to being just.

CHARACTERISTICS OF NATURAL DISPOSITIONS

Natural dispositions contain four important features for life: a source, a purpose, an object, and an impulse. Source refers to the cause that the natural disposition represents and remains the same for each; natural purpose is completion of the perfection of nature in its mode of operation and this remains the same in minerals, plants, animals, and the self. However, the self is free to choose to remember or to choose to forget or to remain unconscious to

---

SOURCE: THE CAUSE THAT THE NATURAL DISPOSITION REPRESENTS.

PURPOSE: COMPLETION OF THE PERFECTION OF NATURE IN ITS MODE OF OPERATION.

OBJECT: INCLUDES ALL THE PREPARATION ONE HAS TO UNDERTAKE IN ORDER TO SATISFY THE OBJECT.

IMPULSE: CHANGES

the purpose of creation; the object of a natural disposition includes all the preparation one has to undertake in order to satisfy the object. Objects may vary because it depends on whether or not what is needed is available. If not, the vital-nervous energies may be displaced again and again until an object that satisfies the natural disposition is found. The impulse of a natural disposition changes.

The affective-behavioral systems attract pleasure and avoid harm; the cognitive system collects internal impulses and external stimuli to which it responds. It also has the potential to consciously regulate the total natural dispositions of the self. The traditional model of natural dispositions is for them to be held in moderation, balance, and equilibrium. The purpose of natural disposition, then, is perfection of nature's mode of operation within the self which is caused to deviate from this purpose through the nurturing process.

CLASSES OF NATURAL DISPOSITIONS

Natural dispositions are categorized as attraction to pleasure, avoidance of harm or pain, and/or cognition which develop out of the animal functions of motivation and perception. They serve to reproduce the individual and human race's survival and its development; to preserve the individual and human race from harm; as well as to allow consciousness of self by having been reminded of the abilities of choice and conscience, thereby keeping the individual and human race in balance and equilibrium.

HOW ENERGY IS DISTRIBUTED AND USED

Personality dynamics signifies the way the self grows and changes thereby referring to how natural, vital, and nervous energies are used by the affective-behavioral-cognitive systems. Survival of the individual and of the race is naturally disposed to be through moderation. If any of the three systems goes to an extreme, the control tower of the cognitive system tries to center it by bringing it in balance and once in balance much less vital-nervous energies are required to operate the self because there is no wastage of energy. Every function operates economically in terms of expenditure of vital and nervous energy. If one system goes to an extreme and becomes temporarily stronger, the other systems arise to bring the first back into balance.

THE FLUID ENERGY OF THE AFFECTIVE-BEHAVIOR-COGNITIVE SYSTEMS

During the early stages of development, before the cognitive system is actualized, the affect-behavior systems use the natural and vital energies for nutrition, growth, and development. They invest energy in objects that appear to fulfill their needs of attracting pleasure and avoiding harm. However, as these two do not function cognitively, when needs are not met, they are given by nature the ability to displace their energy towards another object which may satisfy the need with the help of their parent, eventually learning through observation and imitation and the gradual development of cognition, to become selective and choose that which will satisfy the basic need.

COGNITIVE SYSTEM

The cognitive system receives its energy from the vital energy of the heart distributed into the nervous system whereas the affective system receives only natural energy (veinal) and the behavioral system, only vital energy (arterial). The cognitive system is endowed by nature with the ability to identify and match the mental image arising out of a need with a real perception which will satisfy a natural disposition. Whereas the affective-behavior systems believe the impression of a desired object and an object are one and the same thing, the cognitive system may come to know through learning that the impression and the real object are different and that the impression must conform to something real.

Understanding has different names depending on what it is doing. If it is continuing the work begun by the imagination, its subcategories are reason, discourse, penetration, sagacity, judgment, understanding, free-will—the consequence of the knowing process by which the mind reaches out for the positive. Another way is that of imagination. This functions as follows: when the self seeks the truth by means of contemplation it refers to the cognitive intellect. When the self seeks the positive and having found it, goes forward to free-will in order that the self may follow after the positive disposition or flee from negative ones, it refers to the practical intellect. When free-will in the self covets positive dispositions and carries out what understanding advises, the practical intellect of self becomes the Active Intellect.

IDENTIFICATION

The concept of identification is significant because the more refined it becomes, the more of reality it sees and the goal of psychoethics is to complete the perfection of nature in its mode of operation by helping the self to see things as they really are, to identify them with their Source.

One way to help complete nature's mode of operation is to identify and imitate people who are aware and conscious of the same purpose in life. The earliest model of the process of identification for a monotheist usually proves to be one's parents and religious figures. Through this process, something internal, the purposive goal of perfecting the self's nature so that it can return to its Source as it came, conforms to something external, i.e., parents or a religious figure. When it identifies with others whom it admires and respects because they embody the same purpose in life, it makes some of its own characteristics (internal in that they belong to the self) like those of the other person (s) (external to the self).

The process of identification with persons of equal beliefs is greatly emphasized in the dynamics and developmental theory of psychoethics as one of the best methods for preserving the naturally healthy, psychic self as well as for being able to effect change if an imbalance occurs. When identification takes place with people who exhibit the positive traits of nature and revelation, it can then begin to identify with the divinely infused spirit within.

DISPLACEMENT

The method of restoration of health, once an imbalance or disorder appears, is that of displacement of energy, as *Jihad Phase I: Traditional Guidance and Centering the Self* shows. When there is an over, under, or un-developed aspect of any of the three systems—affective, behavioral, cognitive—the recourse is to displace that negative energy onto a positive one; if this fails to work, the recourse is to displace it with an over or under-developed quality in one of the other systems; if this fails to remove the negative trait, recourse is to displace the energy of one negative trait with the energy of its opposite negative trait; and if this also fails, recourse is to cut-off all vital and nervous energies to the negative trait. When an imbalance develops, descriptions of the negative traits appear very similar to defense mechanisms which the cognitive system then has to overcome.

CONCLUSION

The cognitive system is, by nature, the regulating factor of the self. Guided by nature with the choice to acquire knowledge and to act upon that knowledge within the precepts of nature and revelation or not, when there is an imbalance of the self, the cognitive function's conscience reviles and chides the other function (s) which may be out of balance. This brings about further consciousness in the cognitive system. If the cognitive system itself loses its balance and goes to an extreme of overdevelopment, underdevelopment, or undevelopment, it is the consciousness and awareness of the same system which tries to bring it back into a state of moderation. In order for the self to stay centered, the energy of the cognitive function, acting out of perception and motivation, responds. It may have consciously deliberated and freely choose to complete the perfection of nature in its mode of operation. This choice or response becomes the driving force regulating the external senses, the attraction to pleasure, the avoidance of harm/ pain, and the cognitive's unconscious systems. This forms the dynamics of personality. To wisely regulate the self, the cognitive system must keep both itself, the external senses, and the affective and behavioral forces in moderation. If the cognitive system is not strong enough to do this—showing the reason for psychoethics' emphasis upon learning and gaining knowledge—the result will be negative affect, behavior, or cognition.

If affect becomes too strong, the self may become promiscuous and/or gluttonous, impulsive and self-indulgent as overdevelopment; or full of shame and guilt as underdevelopment; or filled with grief and envy as undeveloped aspects of the affective/emotive system. When the affective system is held in moderation, the self is in a state of temperance and modesty. If the behavioral system dominates the self in a stage of overdevelopment, the self can be described as angry, violent, aggressive, and vindictive; or underdeveloped and cowardly; or undeveloped and gripped by fear. If the cognitive system is out of balance and not able to regulate itself, the self may be overdeveloped and full of deceit, cunning, and trickery and/or a belief system based in hypocrisy; underdeveloped and in a state of preconsciousness, knowing that it does not know and/or a belief system based in multitheism or idolatry; or undeveloped exhibiting unconsciousness where the self does not know and does not know that it does not know and/or a belief system based in disbelief and infidelity to the One God. If the practical intellect, including free-will and conscience, is out of balance, the self is far from being fair and just. When the self is in balance, the practical intellect regulates the self and the self has found certainty in the belief of the One God, monotheism.

PART II:
DEVELOPMENTAL
AND
LEARNING THEORY

5

EVOLUTIONARY DEVELOPMENT OF THE SELF

STAGES OF DEVELOPMENT OF NATURE IN ITS MODE OF OPERATION

Development, based on the ability to receive impressions and forms and then to respond to them, is an important consideration in psychoethics because any disorder that may appear in the self is restored to health in the same natural order as it was created. When the self reflects on guidance in nature, it sees that it is the only creature that is endowed with the capacity to reflect on self and to choose freely to do or not do something. These, the most beautiful gifts of nature in its mode of operation or Divine Will, makes the self special. When the self reflects on *tashri'i* guidance, it realizes that that special quality or gift that it—and only it in all of nature—has is because of the infusion of the Divine Spirit. *Tashri'i* guidance says: "*When I have shaped him/her and breathed My spirit in him/her...*" (15:29) or "*...and breathed His Spirit in him/her,*" (32:9).

Ibn Miskawayh and Nasir al-Din Tusi describes the development of the human being beginning with the mineral soul or nature in its mode of operation in minerals where the four elements and their qualities are preserved. This was discussed in structure and so here we begin with the next stage of development, that of the vegetative stage .

THE VEGETATIVE STAGE

Ibn Miskawayh explains the development of nature's mode of operation in the plant or vegetive soul:

> I DIED FROM MINERAL
>   AND PLANT BECAME;
> DIED FROM THE PLANT
>   AND TOOK A SENTIENT FRAME;
> DIED FROM THE BEAST,
>   AND DONNED A HUMAN
>   DRESS.
> WHEN BY MY DYING DID I
>   E'ER GROW LESS.
> ANOTHER TIME FROM
>   HUMANHOOD I MUST DIE
> TO SOAR WITH ANGEL-PINIONS
>   THROUGH THE SKY.
> 'MIDST ANGELS ALSO I MUST
>   LOSE MY PLACE
> SINCE 'EVERYTHING SHALL
>   PERISH SAVE HIS FACE.'
> LET ME BE NAUGHT! THE
>   HARP-STRINGS TELL ME
>   PLAIN
> THAT UNTO HIM DO WE
>   RETURN AGAIN!
> JALAL AL-DIN RUMI, *MATHNAWI*, TRANS.
> E. G. BROWNE.

If it reaches the point where it receives the form of the plant, it will become, by the addition of this form, superior to any inanimate object. This addition consists of [the powers of] nutrition, of growth, of spreading, and of drawing from the soil and from water what suits its nature, abandoning what does not suit it, and discharging from the body, in the form of gums, the excretions which are formed in it from its food. These are the differences between plants and inanimate objects. They represent a condition added to the mere physical state which exists in the inanimate object.

This additional condition in the plant, by virtue of which it becomes superior to the inanimate object, is of various grades, for certain plants, such as coral and the like, differ only slightly from inanimate objects. Then the plants advance gradually from one grade to another and appropriate more and more of that addition. Thus, some plants grow without cultivation or sowing, fail to preserve their kind by fruits or seeds, and do not need for their formation anything beyond the combination of the elements, winds, and sunshine. That is why they are in the realm of the inanimate objects and akin to them.

Then this quality of the plants is enhanced until there appears in some of them the power of bearing fruit and of preserving their kind by means of seeds through which they produce their like. This condition represents an addition to, and a distinction from, the species that come before them. Then [as we pass from some plants to others], this quality grows further so that the third [species] becomes as superior to the second as the second is to the first, and the [species] becomes as superior to the second as the second is to the first, and the species keep on rising in rank and some surpassing others until they attain the end of their realm and enter that of the animal.

Here are the superior trees such as the olive tree, the pomegranate tree, the vine, and the various fruit-bearing trees. But, even here, the faculties are still mixed—I mean that the faculties of their males and their females are still mixed and not distinct each from the other, that is, these plants bear and re-

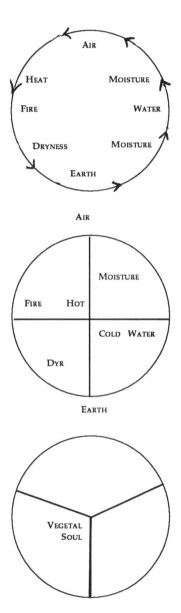

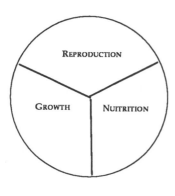

LENGHT   DEPTH   BREADTH

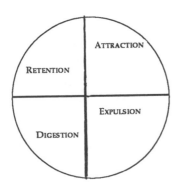

produce their like. They have not yet attained the limit of their realm which joins that of the animal.

But some species advance still further in this realm until they reach the realm of the animal and cannot receive any addition, for any slight addition would make them animals and would take them out of the realm of the plant. Here their faculties become distinct, male and female qualities are produced in them, and they come to possess animal characteristics which distinguish them from the rest of the plants and trees. An example of this is the palm tree which touches the realm of the animal by virtue of the ten properties which are enumerated in [the Natural Sciences]. Only one grade separates it from the animal and that is the capacity to uproot itself from the soil and to go in search of food.

Tradition has preserved an allusion to, or a symbol of, this truth in the words of the Prophet (ص), 'Honor your aunt the palm tree for it was created from the remains of the clay of which Adam was made.' Should a plant develop the capacity to move, to uproot itself from its realm and to seek its food instead of being tied down to its place and having to wait for its food to be brought to it, and should also other organs be formed in it by which it can obtain what it needs to remedy its deficiencies—should a plant develop succapacities, it would become an animal. [1]

THE ANIMAL STAGE

Ibn Miskawayh continues with the development of the animal soul:

REPRODUCTION

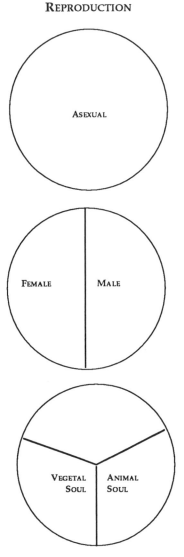

These organs develop in the animal from the beginning of its realm and grow better and some animals become thereby nobler than others—exactly as was the case with plants. They go on achieving one quality after another until they develop the faculty of feeling pleasure and pain. Here the animal is pleased when it attains its benefits and is pained when harms befall it. Then it advances to the stage in which it receives the inspiration of God and thus recognizes what is good for it and what is bad, seeking the former and avoiding the latter. Those animals which stand at the beginning, near the realm of the plant, such as worms, flies, and the lower kinds of insects, do not copulate or beget their kind, but reproduce asexually.

Then the ability to acquire qualities develops in the animals—as was equally the case with the plants. They come to acquire the faculty of anger by which they rise to defend themselves against anything that is harmful. They are given weapons in accordance with their strength and with their ability to use them. If this avoidance of harm/pain disposition is intense, their weapons are powerful and complete; if it is deficient, the weapons are deficient also; and if it is very weak, they are not given any

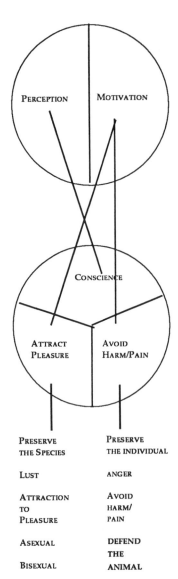

PERCEPTION	MOTIVATION
	CONSCIENCE
ATTRACT PLEASURE	AVOID HARM/PAIN

PRESERVE THE SPECIES	PRESERVE THE INDIVIDUAL
LUST	ANGER
ATTRACTION TO PLEASURE	AVOID HARM/ PAIN
ASEXUAL	DEFEND THE
BISEXUAL	ANIMAL

weapons at all, but are merely equipped with the means to flee, such as swiftness in running and the ability to use cunning to escape dangers.

You can see this clearly when you observe the animal that is equipped with horns which serve it as spears, the one that is given teeth and claws which serve it as knives and daggers, the one that possesses a shooting organ which serves it as darts and arrows, and the one that is equipped with hoofs which serve it as a mace or a battle-ax.

Concerning the animals that are not given any weapons at all, this is because of their inability to use them, their lack of courage, the deficiency of their avoidance of harm system, and because, should they have been given them, such weapons would have become a burden to them. These animals (such as hares, foxes, and the like) are equipped with means which serve them to flee or to deceive, like swiftness in running, agility, craftiness, and cunning. And if you examine carefully the conditions of such existents as beasts of prey, wild animals, and birds, you will find this wise law constant in all of them. Blessed be God, the Supreme Creator.

Those animals that find their way to copulation, the begetting of offspring, the protection and bringing up of the young, and the concern to keep them safe in a shelter, nest, or den (as we observe in those that reproduce and lay eggs) and finally to feed them, either with their milk or with the food that they bring to them—such animals are superior to those that are not able to do any of these things. Then these conditions are enhanced among the animals until some of them come close to the realm of the human being. Here they become responsive to training and, as such, superior to other animals. This quality goes on growing so that some animals become thereby pre-eminent in various ways, as in the case of the horse and the trained falcon.

Finally we pass from this rank to the rank of the animals which imitate the human being of their own accord and follow his example without any instruction, such as apes and the like. These attain such a degree of intelligence that it is only necessary for them, in order to be trained, to see a person perform a certain act and then to do something like it, without giving the human being any trouble or obliging him to discipline them. This is the furthest point in the animal realm. If any animal crosses it and receives a slight addition, it will leave this realm and pass to the realm of the human being. [2]

PHYSICAL WEAPONS OF DEFENSE
HORNS/SPEARS
TEETH & CLAWS'
DAGGERS
SHOOTING ORGAN/ DARTS
HOOFS/MACE

NON-PHYSICAL WEAPONS OF DEFENSE
AGILITY
DECEPTION

THE STAGE OF THE HUMAN SOUL OR SELF

The human being is capable of acquiring intelligence, discernment, and rationality, the organs which these capacities use, and the forms which are appropriate to them. When he attains this rank, he proceeds towards knowledge and acquires functions, capacities, and gifts from God which enable him to progress and advance as was the case with the other ranks which we have described. [3]

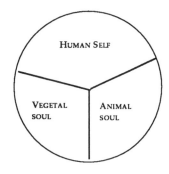

CONCLUSION

The self, then, is the continuation of the process of nature in its mode of operation. It contains the infusion of the Divine Spirit along with the processes of nature in its mode of operation developed in the mineral, plant, and animal "soul," as well as the highest stage—that of consciousness of self.

NOTES TO EVOLUTIONARY DEVELOPMENT OF THE SELF

1 Ibn Miskawayh, p. 45. See Glossary.
2 *Ibid.*, p. 52.
3 *Ibid.*, p. 54.

6
LEARNING THEORY

STAGE OF AFFECT OR ATTRACTION TO PLEASURE

Learning theory in the traditional perspective follows exactly upon the developmental theory as the unfolding of nature in its mode of operation. Following the natural course, learning should enhance the possibility of becoming centered. A child first learns how to attract pleasure and then how to avoid harm. Naturally disposed towards cognition, the applications of cognition are learned through the nurturing process.

Dawwani describes the stages of learning in his *Akhlaq-i-Jalali* :

Now when we consider the succession of the powers, it is clear that the first engendered in the infant is the power of seeking for sustenance: for in a single hour from its birth it manifests

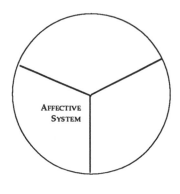

an inclination to suck which it can only derive by natural disposition from the Almighty: according to the text, '*He gave everything its nature and instruction moreover to the smallest of beings.*' In the course of this 'attraction to pleasure,' as his strength increases, crying and the like becomes associated with its relief. Whereto, in the first instance, being engrossed by the generic feeling, he is unable to distinguish between things so similar as the person of his mother and of other people: afterwards, as the senses external and internal gather strength, and the mind becomes equal to retaining the image of the thing perceived, the shapes of objects reaching him by the channel of sense and with them the severalty of his mother and other people are sufficiently apprehended. [1]

STAGE OF BEHAVIORAL OR AVOIDANCE OF HARM/PAIN

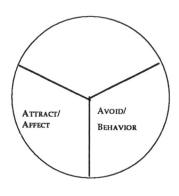

Next after the perfection of this power (in one stage of its perfection) the 'avoidance of harm/pain' makes its appearance by which he is to repel whatever is injurious to him, and resist whatever molests or opposes him in his 'attraction to pleasure' after the objects of want and desire; or, if himself is unequal to avoiding them, he is to seek support and assistance by appealing and referring to others. [2]

STAGE OF COGNITION OR DISCERNMENT

After the perfection of this power (in one stage of perfection), the cognitive system, which is the power of discerning, develops itself; and the first mark of its development is the conscience, which is inferring a difference between positive and negative traits. This however is a system that advances but gradually on the confines of perfection; for it is not until the 'attraction to pleasure' and 'avoidance of harm' powers have by these means brought the individual to his due perfection that they exercise their functions for the preservation of the species.

For example, when the original power productive of nourishment and growth has brought the individual near to the requisite perfection, he becomes possessed of another, by means of which he is to perpetuate his species; then it is that the seminal matter is engendered with the lust for connection and longing for children consequent upon it. The second power, again, when it has been set at rest, and raised above the safeguard of the individual, proceeds to adopt for the family the authority of laws, judicatures, and fraternities; whereby the greatest of benefits result to the species. As to the third power, it is not until he is used to the contemplation of particulars that he begins to comprehend universals, or to figure things in their genera and species.

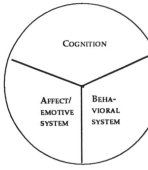

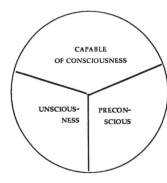

Now it is not until it so generalizes that the name of intellect can be properly applied to it or that there is any approach to development in the distinguishing perfections of the human race: then it is, in fact, that humanization may be said to commence; and to apply the name human to him in his previous state, is like calling datelings and grapelings, dates and grapes. Perfection in this sense, depending on the regulation of the passionate nature, will properly commence with its conscious regulation; increasing as it approaches the true perfection, which is the highest of all degrees accessible to the human being, and has been designated for the vice-gerent of God upon earth.

By this rule then is the aspirant after perfection to regulate his rise. First, from the instinct of the 'attraction to pleasure,' let him acquire the attribute of temperance; next, from the instinct of the 'avoidance of harm,' courage; and lastly, after perfecting the nature of these in himself, let him crown the whole with wisdom. [Once these three are in moderation, justice follows]. If, then, at the outset of his progress he chances to be trained in the course of wisdom, great is the advantage and momentous the gift in gratitude for which his best exertions to preserve these qualities would be but a due return. But if he has been brought up contrariwise, he is not to despond, but persevere in his endeavor to apprehend and overtake it. Let him reflect, that except such as are aided by God, and whom the Almighty, by perfecting in conformation and elevating in intellect, according to the text, *"He found thee going astray and gave thee guidance,"* (93:7) has exempted from the labors of attainment and the pursuits of ordinary life, no one is formed to excellence, or independent of labor in its acquirement; although, doubtless, as they differ in capacity, people proportionally differ in the ease or difficulty with which it may be obtained.

In the same way, then, as persons desirous to attain the art of composition or carpentry must apply themselves to practice, in order to become composers or carpenters, must he who aspires after positive traits betake himself, if he would obtain it, to such practices as are means of originating those dispositions. Now the art in question bears an exact resemblance to medicine: inasmuch as it is the object of the physician to maintain the equilibrium of temperament, as long as it will last, and to restore it when subverted; and the object of the metaphysician is to maintain the equilibrium of disposition, as long as it will endure, and to regain it afterwards. Indeed, this science [psychoethics] is strictly that of mental therapeutics. Like medicine which has two divisions, the maintenance of health and the expulsion of disease, this art has also its two divisions, one applying to the maintenance of positive traits, and the other purporting to avoid or extinguish nega-

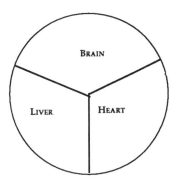

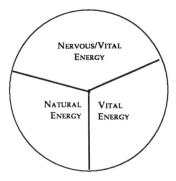

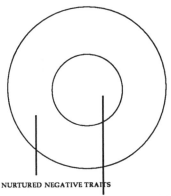

NURTURED NEGATIVE TRAITS

NATURAL DISPOSITION TO POSITIVE TRAITS

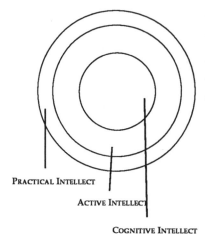

PRACTICAL INTELLECT

ACTIVE INTELLECT

COGNITIVE INTELLECT

tive traits and recover the positive ones. In the outset then the student's view is to be directed summarily to the fundamental condition of the power in their pre-explained succession; and if the condition of each of them agrees with the rule of equilibrium, his only endeavor will be to maintain it. But if perversion has taken place, his business is to bring it back to equilibrium and that pursuant to their order in production. Then, when the powers have been duly effected, he is to bestow his utmost attention to maintaining the principles of equity making it, in fact, the purpose of all his practices and fortunes, until he arrives at the limit of true perfection. [3]

Nasir al-Din Tusi explains how the self is prepared for centering:

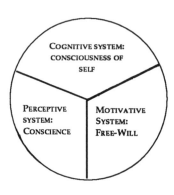

COGNITIVE SYSTEM: CONSCIOUSNESS OF SELF

PERCEPTIVE SYSTEM: CONSCIENCE

MOTIVATIVE SYSTEM: FREE-WILL

When, however, the human self is directed away from what causes deficiency and corruption, reason and rationality come into play and the person then seeks knowledge and learning. The more of these qualities that the human being seeks, so does this quality and characteristic in him increase. The metaphor is given that the faculty of discernment is like a fire which will not light unless the area be free of moisture. Once ignited, however, it grows stronger with every moment and it burns stronger until it fulfills the requirements of its own nature. [4]

CONCLUSION

At the time of birth, a child has the potential for distinguishing between what is pleasure and what is pain. If children are guided through nature and revelation in their encounters with their home, school, and/or work, environment, by having been oriented towards preserving psychic health, the child at puberty, using the cognitive system to the extent it has been actualized, can distinguish between positive and negative traits in terms of being able to perfect his or her divinely created nature. The child develops its potential for rationality, a potential that the affect and behavior systems lack, which it uses to distinguish between what *takwini* and *tashri'i* guidance have taught it and what its natural dispositions need as opposed to what they demand. Demands or compulsions signify to the cognitive system that irrational forces are at work and need to be regulated if the person is going to be able to perfect his nature by the time of the return to the creative source. The cognitive system, when in a state of equilibrium, neither inhibits the naturally disposed forces nor forces moral goals on itself because it operates at the level of free-will and as the Quran says: *"there is no compulsion in the Way of Life (din, religion)."* Even though the self is free to choose to do or not to do, it is held answerable for that choice. It uses reason and rationality to understand what is real and reality.

Nasir al-Din Tusi elaborates on the process of centering:

The human being should control his will and his quest for his own interests in the sensible world as well as the sensory things relating to self and body, and whatever is joined to the one or associated with the other. Moreover, the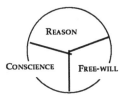

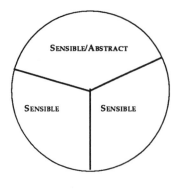

control of sensible states should not de-
part from an equilibrium agreeable to
those states. But in this state, the human
being's nature is still involved with passions and desires except he preserve in
the equilibrium and avoid excess. In
such a position he is closer to what he
should perform than to that from which
he must refrain; for his affairs are directed towards a mean, regulatory rightness
in positive disposition, not falling outside the determining of reflection, albeit
mingled with the control of sensibles.[5]

Variation is accounted for by the following reasons:

VARIATIONS BASED ON:
NATURE
CUSTOMS
KNOWELDGE
UNDERSTANDING
ASPIRATIONS
MOTIVATION TO CHANGE

...the variance of natures; the variance
of customs; the discrepancy in the as-
cending degrees of science, knowledge,
and understanding; the variance of as-
pirations; in conformity with the discrepancy in yearning and in bearing the
toil of the quest. [6]

Ibn Miskawayh sums up the process:

When the self reaches the limit of its
realm, it touches the beginning of the
realm of the angels. This is the highest
rank possible for the human being.
Here the existents are unified and their
beginnings become joined to their ends
and vice versa. This is called the circle
of unity, for the circle is that which has
been defined as one line which moves
from a certain point and ends at it. The
circle of unity is the unified circle which

creates unity out of multiplicity and which is a correct and demonstrative proof of the unity, wisdom, power, and munificence of its Creator.

If now you imagine and understand as much as we have alluded to, you will realize the condition for which you were created and to which you are summoned, the realm which touches your own, and your advancement from one rank and one class to another. You will have genuine faith. You will be able to progress gradually to the noble and hidden sciences, beginning with the study of logic, which is the instrument for the correction of understanding and of instinctive reason. You will proceed with the help of this science to earn the knowledge of all the creatures and of their natures, and then to become attached to this knowledge, to advance in it, and to attain thereby the divine sciences. Here you will be ready to receive the facts and gifts of God. His divine grace will descend upon you and you will be free from the agitation of nature and its movements towards animal passions. You will note the ranks of the existents through which you evolved gradually and you will know that each one of the ranks could not have existed without the preceding ones. You will know also that the self does not achieve its perfection of nature in its mode of operation until it has passed through all that lies before him and that when the self becomes perfected and reaches the end of its realm.... it will become an in-

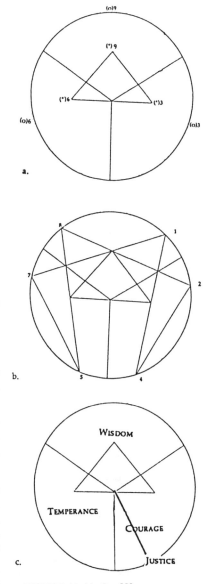

a = UNITY divided by 3 = .333
 1/3 + 1/3 = .666
 1/3 + 1/3 + 1/3 = .999
b = UNITY divided by 7 = .142857 (a recurring decimal with no 3, 6, or 9 in it.
c = 3 systems (cognitive, affective, behavioral) times 4 positive traits of temperance, courage, wisdom and justice.

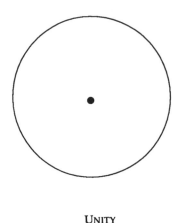

UNITY
CENTEREDNESS

termediary between the higher world and the lower, as a result of its conception of the conditions of all existents and of the condition to which it is promoted from the merely human one and as a result of sighting the realms which we have described. Then, also, it will understand the words of God, "No self knows what delight of the eyes is hidden in reserve for them." And it will realize the meaning of the saying of Muhammad (ﷺ), "There, there is what no eye has ever seen, nor an ear ever heard, nor ever occurred to the heart of a human being."[7]

And Nasir al-Din Tusi adds:

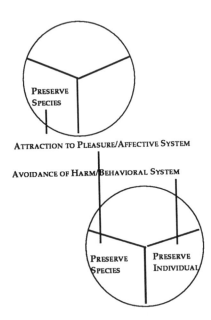

PRESERVE
SPECIES

ATTRACTION TO PLEASURE/AFFECTIVE SYSTEM

AVOIDANCE OF HARM/BEHAVIORAL SYSTEM

PRESERVE
SPECIES

PRESERVE
INDIVIDUAL

As each one of these faculties reaches a perfection possible according to the individual, he concerns himself in any way feasible with the observance of that perfection in the species. As to the first faculty, which is the principle of the attraction of what is pleasurable, and the one entrusted with the nurture of the individual, when it has brought the individual (by nourishing and development) close to the perfection towards which he is directed, he becomes excited to preserve the species; hence arise a passion for mating and a longing for procreation. As for the second faculty, namely the principle of avoiding whatever is harmful, when it becomes fully able to preserve the individual, it proceeds to protect the species; thus becomes apparent a yearning for favors and all manner of ascendancy and dominion. As for the third faculty, the principle of reason and distinction, when it has found skill in the perception of individuals and particulars, it occupies itself with the intellection of species and universals, receiving the name of 'intelligence'. In this state, it becomes in very fact a recipient of the name 'humanity', and the perfection entrusted to the regulation of nature becomes complete.[8]

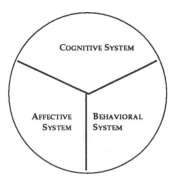

NOTES TO LEARNING THEORY

1 Dawwani, p. 42.
2 *Ibid.*, p. 43.
3 *Ibid.*, p. 43.
4 Tusi, p. 89.
5 *Ibid.*, p. 89.
6 *Ibid.*, p. 90.
7 *Ibid.*, p. 91.
8 *Ibid.*, p. 91.

PART III

7

RESEARCH
AND EVALUATION

INTRODUCTION

The traditional personality paradigm opens up numerous areas of research and study showing its heuristic value. However any research done should be done and undertaken with the same ethical basis as that of the initial personality paradigm to bring about a fair scientific evaluation of it, that is, to study and observe it as a Divine Trust.

Modern psychology and psychotherapy are clearly delineated along the lines of cognitive, affective, behavioral, or some combination of them with perception and motivation as underlying dynamics of approach to personality because of their very generic qualities. The traditional personality paradigm also focuses on these three systems which develop in the personality out of perception and motivation. Any research done to date in any of these areas which confirms the presence of one of these systems has already verified the paradigm and can be adopted into it in much the same way that the scientific observations of human nature by the early Greeks was adopted into psychoethics.

There are some aspects of the traditional personality paradigm which cannot be proven or disproven like the immortality of an aspect of the human self—the conscious aspect of its cognitive system—that which was breathed into it through the Divine Spirit. Psychologists tend to reject a divinely-inspired system because of this and yet there are many areas in the various present personality theories like those of Freud, Jung, and so forth that have not been verified by experiment so this should not be a reason for rejection of this personality paradigm.

On the other hand, there are many aspects of this personality paradigm which can be verified or disproven by scientific research. As a beginning step, an instrument is being devised by the author to test an adult's position in terms of moderation in regard to wisdom, temperance, and courage to be able to predict adult behavior of fairness and justice in the work place, in schools, within the family environment, in terms of substance abuse and so forth.

RESEARCH QUESTIONS

It could be asked: Is the self a development of nature in its mode of operation? Questions on the Developmental Theory could include experiments that have to a large extent already been done in the area of development of the self through the stages of what is traditionally seen as the plant, animal, and human stage or nature in its mode of operation to show its evolution but rather than concluding that the human being developed from the ape, they would see, rather, the gradual evolution of the inner self as the evolution of nature in its mode of operation and not the outer form. The learning theory of the traditional personality paradigm can be tested in the classrooms by teachers who already have been taught the basics of the paradigm but it was done as if one were studying the branch of a tree rather than looking at education from the Divine roots.

Questions in regard to positive and negative traits in this personality paradigm could be asked. On the negative side, questions that could be asked in light of this paradigm include: Does anger develop out of an overdevelopment of avoidance of pain? Are these the only causes of anger? Are these the only consequences? Does fear develop out of an undeveloped avoidance of pain system? Does cowardice develop from an underdevelopment of the human instinct of avoidance of pain? Does promiscuity as a negative trait lead a person away from education and seeking knowledge and into disease and possibly early death because of the rapid extinction of vital energy? Or not? Is promiscuity an overdevelopment of a sense of modesty? Does envy develop because of an undevelopment of the attraction to pleasure human instinct? Do laziness, sloth, and idleness develop from an underdeveloped sense of attraction to pleasure? Is a state of preconsciousness of God and His creation an undevelopment of human reasoning power? If so, what does this imply? If not, what is it? Does deceit develop out of an overdevelopment of reason? How can one deal with unconsciousness whereby a person does not know and does not know that he does not know?

Questions could be asked in regard to Divine Guidance in human nature and acquired guidance through revelation. Questions could be asked in regard to the role of Prophets like Moses (ع), Jesus (ع), and Muhammad (ص) as models for social learning in light of this personality paradigm: Questions in regard to the goal of the self could be asked. And finally, it needs to be asked if human beings actually do obtain happiness and well-being, at least in this life, if they base their life on this paradigm? Does it help them perfect their human nature? Is this an effective method of living a fuller, richer life considering the fact that no one can become centered unless another human being gain from the positive traits that they have developed?

EVALUATION

The traditional personality paradigm has been evaluated and proven in its various parts by psychologists. Rational emotive theory, behavioral theory, cognitive theory, psychodynamic theory, humanistic theory — all have looked at a part, but overlooked the paradigm that serves as the origin for each one of the theories. Practiced as psychoethics for centuries, perhaps the time has come to research the monotheistic paradigm itself in regard to personality, development, and learning theory.

PART IV

8
CONCLUSION

The self operates out of three basic systems. The first of the three to form is the "attraction to pleasure." Next is the "avoidance of pain," and, finally, the cognitive system. These three are equivalent to the three souls mentioned in the Quran. The *nafs al-ammarah* (12:53)or animal soul is the affective/ behavioral systems. The *nafs al-lawwamah* (75:2)or self-reproaching soul refers to the cognitive system. When all three function in moderation under the regulation of consciousness from the cognitive system, the self is called "the soul at peace," *nafs al-muta'minah*. (89:27)

The animal aspects of self ensures the enduring quality of the physical form which acts as the vehicle of the cognitive self during the time in which it realizes its perfection and reaches its goal. The function of the *nafs al-lawwamah* is to regulate the *nafs al-ammarah* so as to ward off the negative traits that develop when either the affective or behavioral systems gain dominance. It is the affective/behavioral systems which unite with free-will to either command the self to indulgence in desires like eating, lust, etc. or to power and aggression in states like that of anger. The self-reproaching soul reproaches and repents. When all three are in a state of moderation, regulated by consciousness, the peaceful soul is born which possesses discipline and generosity in both reality and substance.

The cognitive system is the highest system in the development of nature in its mode of operation of the self. It consists of a practical intellect which regulates actions and contains the cognitive intellect which consists of the potential, habitual, Active, and acquired intellects.

The self is born with the practical intellect which at birth actualizes into the potential intellect. As the self grows, when part of a nurturing process that seeks to preserve a healthy self, from puberty onwards, through good habits and self-discipline, the habitual intellect evolves. The cognitive intellect, at this point, has acquired knowledge and possessed it—that is, it has passed from potentiality to actuality.

When the habitual intellect is caused by the exercise of free-will—the highest form of motivation in nature's mode of operation—to reflect upon itself, it distinguishes between the positive and negative traits through its conscience—the highest form of perception of nature in its mode of operation. The practical intellect has completed its perfection by actualizing the cognitive intellect within the self with the aid of the Active Intellect, becoming what is referred to as the acquired intellect. The self is now capable of knowing self.

The conscience-free-will aspects of the practical intellect, working with the Active Intellect which causes it to reflect, have actualized the cognitive intellect, the highest level of which is that of understanding. The combination of conscience-free-will-understanding lead to consciousness of self. Once this is activated through the acquisition process, the self comes into full play. It seeks knowledge in order to know the self of which it has now become conscious. The previous practical now Active Intellect, locus of conscience, free-will, and consciousness of self now freely chooses what it was naturally disposed to know between positive and negative traits. It seeks to polish the mirror of self by cleansing the rust that has covered nature in its mode of operation's natural disposition of the self by regulating the irrational processes within. The irrational processes consist of the unconscious, preconscious, and overconscious aspects of self. The unconscious processes include the affective system and an undevelopment of the cognitive system. The preconscious processes within the self include the behavioral system and an underdevelopment of the cognitive system. The overconscious process relates solely to the cognitive system and is considered to be an extreme of it.

The Active Intellect is naturally disposed not to allow the irrational forces to get the upper hand. By regulating what is lower, it must be able to receive what is higher, as well, namely knowledge from the cognitive intellect. The cognitive intellect is naturally disposed to *takwini* guidance, but once habitual, it can freely choose *tashri'i* guidance, as well. As the self begins to cleanse away the rust which has accumulated in negative traits hiding the reflective capacity of the positive ones, when the self is accompanied by Divine Assistance, it begins to read the Signs on the horizon and sees that they correspond to the Signs within. This correspondence serves as the basis for learning the Sign language for further guidance. This time the guidance is acquired by free-will because of the presence of Divine Assistance. The self knows itself and its weaknesses and imperfections. It knows such weakness and imperfection could never have been the cause of the perfection of nature in its mode of operation. Once it learns the Sign language of revelation (*tashri'i* guidance), it then sees

Reality and comes to have certainty about things as they really are.

Developed through a nurturing process that seeks to preserve the healthy self by freely accepting *takwini* and *tashri'i* guidance, the self has become conscious. Through the process of the practical intellect's evolution into that of the Active Intellect, the self now wants to know who it is. In seeking that which is real, guided by the Signs upon the horizon and within the 'self', it comes to realize the Real, the Truth.

Looking at nature and its mode of operation, it realizes that the natural state is one of balance and order, that all of nature is centered through *takwini* guidance. It realizes that nothing else in nature can become conscious of self. It is reminded through *tashri'i* guidance of the covenant and the trust that it accepted in return for which it received the potential perfection of nature in its mode of operation: consciousness of self. It, too, wants to be centered and in balance and harmony within itself. It reflects again on itself and sees that negative traits are keeping it off balance, preventing it from being centered. It freely chooses (*takwini* guided) to allow deliberation, understanding, and reason (*takwini* and *tashri'i* guided) to regulate the self by reminding it of its original nature. The self seeks centeredness in order to carry out the trusteeship of nature that it accepted when the Creator created the process of creation, that is, nature in its mode of operation By becoming 'centered', it naturally deals with fairness and justice in its relationships to God, to nature including other human beings, and to self.

It centers itself in wisdom, temperance, and courage by consciously developing traits that serve to regulate unconscious, preconscious, and overconscious traits. When the self senses centeredness, it tests its reality by benefiting others. Without this test, it cannot attain centeredness When another benefits from this, then the self has passed the test and needs only to remain conscious of it so as not to lose the ground it has gained. According to psychoethics, it is then that the self can be called a microcosm of the macrocosmic universe. It is then that the self feels responsible for the trust and executes it with justice. It is then that the self becomes committed to counseling others to positive traits and to preventing negative ones and this is just Phase I of the Greater Jihad.

Glossary

Affective System: The affective/emotive system, known as "the attraction to pleasure: is the most basic of the three major psychological systems of the self. It forms one of the two parts of the *nafs al-ammarah* or animal soul referred to in the Quran (12: 53).

Algazel or al-Ghazali is considered to be one of the greatest thinkers not only in Muslim philosophy, but in human thought, as well. His work influenced Jewish thinkers like Maimonides (d. 1204) who wrote in Arabic and derived his knowledge of Greek philosophy from Arabic translations. Christian thinkers did not remain without influence from Algazel as well. The Dominican Raymund Martin was thoroughly acquainted with Algazel's major works as was his contemporary, Thomas Acquinas (d. 1274). Algazel is considered to be the best known writer on moral subjects. His spread and influence on the Islamic world in this area may be seen through two of his works, namely *Mizan al-'Amal* (Criterion of Action) and *Ihya Ulum al-Din* (Revival of the Religious Sciences), both of which are referred to in this present work.

Amr bi'l ma'ruf: See Counseling to Positive Traits.

Attraction to Pleasure: See Affective System.

Avempace (d. 1138): Abu Bakr Muhammad ibn Yahya al-Sa'igh, known as Ibn Bajjah, developed the psychology of Avicenna and al-Ghazali, expanding on the internal sense of imagination.

Averroes (b. 1126): Abu al-Walid Muhammad ibn Ahmad ibn Muhammad ibn Rushd is well-known for his commentaries on Aristotle and his further refinement of the cognitive and practical intellects.

Avicenna: Abu Ali al-Husayn ibn Abdullah ibn Sina (d. 1037). Avicenna deals more with psychology than with ethics but because he deals so extensively with psychology, he becomes an important source for psychoethics. In terms of psychology, he sees the self as the evolutionary completion of the vegetal and animal souls and then the acquisition of consciousness. His views serve as the basis for the psychological aspect of this work. In regard to ethics, he develops the four positive dispositions of Plato. Three of them, namely, wisdom, courage, and temperance correspond to the rational or cognitive, avoidance of harm or behavioral and attraction to pleasure or affective system. When these positive traits attain moderation, justice ensures. Justice, then, does not have the two extremes as the other positive traits do.

Avoidance of Harm/Pain: See Behavioral System

Behavioral System: The behavioral system, known as avoidance of harm/pain is the second of the three psychological systems of the self to evolve. It forms one part of the two parts of the *nafs al-ammarah* referred to in the Quran (12:53).

Centeredness: Centeredness takes place when the self is kept in moderation by the cognitive system in temperance, courage, and wisdom, thereby becoming a just person if and only if another benefits from one's such moderation.

Cognitive System: This is the last of the three major psychological systems of the self to form. Known in philosophy as reason or rationality, in psychoethics it is called cognition. It is referred to as the *nafs al-lawwamah* or self-reproaching soul in the Quran (75:2).

Conscience: Regulation of free-will comes by its freely accepting to listen to the advice of its conscience when it is regulated by reason. Conscience is the highest level or perfection of perception by nature in its mode of operation.

Consciousness: The ability to consciousness has been granted to the human being alone because of its accepting the covenant with God and the trust of nature. It was infused into the human self as the Divine Breathe or Spirit and is the highest form of perfection of the evolutionary development of nature. Nature, however, developed it in potentia. According to psychoethics, it is up to the individual to complete the perfection that nature has provided by becoming conscious of self or coming to know self. To do so is to complete God's Will. Thus, one who is conscious of self becomes conscious of God the Creator-Guide. It is then that it can be said, "God's Will Is Done."

Counseling to Positive Traits: Known as *amr bi'l ma'ruf*, this religious command becomes obligatory, according to psychoethics, when one has centered the self. The other half of the command is to prevent the development of negative traits (*nahy an al-munkar*) within the self and others.

Dawwani, Muhammad ibn As'ad Jalal al-Din. Dawwani (d. 1501) revised the *Akhlaq-i-Nasiri* of Tusi, adding the relevant Quranic verses and Traditions of the Prophet. His most famous work on ethics is called *Akhlaq-i-Jalali*. Dawwani's ethical theory is based on the position of the human being as the vice-gerent of God on earth. For Dawwani, the struggle towards completing the perfection of nature in its mode of operation presupposes that every and any disposition is capable of positive change if constant vigilance is maintained after a positive learning experience.

Developmental Theory: According to psychoethics, the human self evolved out of the completion of the perfection of nature in its mode of operation which begins with the elements (earth, air, fire, and water) and their qualities (hot, cold, moisture, dryness), moves through the plant stage (assimilation, growth, reproduction) to the animal stage (motivation, perception) and finally to the self which is infused with the Divine Spirit when it is granted the ability to become conscious of self.

Disposition: A disposition may be either natural or acquired. The natural disposition or *fitrat* is a positive, healthy self. It is through the nurturing process that unhealthy dispositions develop.

Fitrat: See Disposition, natural.

Free-will: Psychoethics is basically concerned with learning to regulate the free-will actions of the human being through reason or cognition. Free-will is the highest level or perfection of motivation by nature in its mode of operation.

Greater Jihad: The Greater Jihad in the Way of God or struggle with the self (*jihad al-akbar*) is considered to be much more difficult than any outward struggle.

Habit: Habit is described as the continuous repetition of certain acts which may be positive or negative.

Hadi: Guide, one of the Names of God, this is the closest concept to that of the counselor therapist in the West.

Hanif: A *hanif* is a monotheist. See monotheism.

Ibn Miskawayh (d. 1030). Ahmad ibn Muhammed ibn Ya'qub. For this man, known as the first Muslim moralist, psychology and ethics were so interconnected that he begins his famous treatise on ethics, *Tahdhib al-Akhlaq*, with psychology and the soul. It is a tradition followed by the major exponents of practical philosophy who followed him. Following Plato, he makes the connection between the three positive traits and the three-systems of the self, namely, cognitive, affective, and behavioral. From their balance comes justice.

Intellect: The highest level or perfection of nature in its mode of operation in the cognitive system, from out of the intellect arises consciousness of self leading to consciousness of God as Creator-Guide. See Cognitive System.

Jihad Phase I: Traditional Guidance and Centering the Self: This forthcoming volume develops the theory of Muslim counseling based on the monotheistic personality paradigm of *God's Will Be Done*.

Jihad Phase II: According to psychoethics, once a person is centered in temperance, courage, and wisdom and has benefited another, thereby becoming a just person, that person has succeeded in holding the self in moderation through the use of reason and the cognitive system. Once this is accomplished, the person is ready to continue to the second phase of the journey. This phase of the Greater Jihad rejects reason and the rationality it has so diligently learned and relies solely on intuition operating out of the imagination to spiral on its return to the One from whence it has come.

Learning Theory: According to psychoethics, the child first develops the attraction to pleasure and then avoidance of harm/pain functions. The last of the three major functions to develop is that of cognition which goes through four stages within the cognitive intellect: potential, habitual, Active, and acquired. The last two stages happen after puberty.

Monotheism: This is the world view which forms the basis for the Semitic religions of Judaism, Christianity, and Islam. The belief in One God is strongest in the Jewish and Islamic traditions. See Preface for a description of monotheism.

Motivation: Motivation arises out of the animal soul and along with perception marks the distinction between animals and plants.

Mushrik: A religious person who believes in too many gods from the monotheist perspective. See Preface for a description of this person's world view.

Nafs al-ammarah. See Affective System and Behavioral System.

Nafs al-lawwamah. See Cognitive System.

Nafs al-muta'minah: See Cognitive System.

Nahy an al-munkar: See Counseling to Positive Traits.

Naraqi, Muhammad Mahdi ibn Abi Dharr (d. early 19th century) is the author of an important work in ethics entitled *Jami al-Sa'adat* (Collector of Felicities) Written in Arabic and published in three volumes, it is compendium of the treatises on ethics which preceded him, namely the *Akhlaq-i-Nasiri* of Nasir al-Din Tusi.

Nature in its Mode of Operation: The connection between nature and the self is not through the physical form but through the creative process operative in nature. This creative process may also be seen as *takwini* guidance and in traditional psychoethics it is referred to as the soul (*nafs*) and is regarded as being the Will of God flowing through all of creation.

Negative Traits or Dispositions: These are called vices in philosophy and they correspond to negative traits or dispositions in psychoethics.

Perception: Perception arises out of the animal soul and along with motivation marks the distinction between animals and plants.

Positive Traits or Dispositions: These are called virtues in philosophy and they correspond to positive traits or dispositions in psychoethics.

Practical Philosophy: Practical philosophy is that branch of philosophy which traditionally deals with ethics, economics, and politics.

Preventing the Development of Negative Traits: See Counseling to Positive Traits.

Psychoethics: Traditional psychology is based in ethics and therefore this author has developed the term "psychoethics" to name the unity that developed traditionally between psychology and ethics. Western psychology, on the other hand, developed from the science of medicine and was always closely allied with the concept of the humors, a concept which was rejected in the West with the development of modern psychology. The history of psychology in the Islamic world separated early from the concept of the humors and developed out of the science of ethics. The implications of this phenomena for the modern world are tremendous.

Rhazes, Abu Bakr Muhammad ibn Zakariya al-Razi (d. 925), best known as a physician, his works were known in the Middle Ages. According to A. J. Arberry, Rhazes' work, *Hawi*, was translated into Latin under the title *Continens* by Faraj ibn Salim, A Sicilian Jew in 1279. The extensive work was printed five times between 1488-1542. Arberry has translated a work of Rhazes which represents popular ethics, so much a part of psychoethics.

Self: Often called soul, the self is a single substance capable of a multiplicity of operations. In terms of psychology, it consists of three basic systems: the affective, the behavioral, and the cognitive.

Sign (s): The word *ayah* in Arabic means sign and each of the 6000 some verses of the Quran are called Signs. *Tashri'i* guidance tells the monotheist that the Creator has sent Signs upon the horizon (all of nature) and within themselves (psychoethics) by which they can come to know that God is the Real, the Truth, This, however, requires the ability to be able to read the Signs and then to learn to live by them. Psychoethics developed to help teach the monotheist how to read the Signs and then how to discipline the self to learn to live by them.

Takwini: Innate or instinctive guidance, this type of guidance is universal to all of nature including the human being.

Tashri'i: Acquired guidance based on guidance through the commands of revelation, this is considered to be guidance through nurture.

Tawhid: See monotheism.

Traditional Psychology: Developed from the study of the Signs within and studied as the Science of Ethics, traditional psychology has historically been a branch of Practical Philosophy.

Trait: A disposition that becomes embedded within the self through habit—positive or negative—is called a trait.

Tusi, Nasir al-Din (b. 1201): Tusi was born in Tus less than 100 years after Algazel's death. Tus is also the city where Ghazali spent much of his life and is buried. In his work on ethics, Tusi follows much of Ibn Miskawayh's (d. 1030) *Tahdhib al-Akhlaq*. The ultimate happiness for both of them is the main goal of ethics and this is determined by a person's place in the cosmic evolution. This, in turn, is realized only through discipline and submission to the Will of God by completing the perfection of nature in its mode of operation. Both Tusi and Ibn Miskawayh refer to the Platonic virtues of wisdom, courage, temperance, and justice which are derived from the three-fold division of the self: attraction to pleasure, avoidance of harm, and the intellect which are similar in Aristotle's thought. Aristotle saw disorders or negative traits (vices) as an extreme of positive traits (virtues) and extremes that fall on either side of the moderate mean by an excess or deficit. Ibn Miskawayh follows the same system which gives eight basic negative traits and four basic positive ones. Tusi then develops the thought further. He saw psychoethical disorders as deviation of the self from balance. Aristotle and Miskawayh had seen these disorders in terms of quantity— excess or deficit. The overdevelopment or underdevelopment of a positive trait for them were causes of imbalance. Tusi was the first to express the view that psychoethical disorders are not only quantitative, but qualitative, as well. This third possibility is referred to in this work as undevelopment. As a result, psychoethical disorders may have one of three causes: an overdevelopment of the positive trait, an underdevelopment of it or an undevelopment, the latter alone being a question of imbalance in quality. These three may exist in anyone of the three systems, according to Tusi, that is, in cognition, in affect (attraction to pleasure) or in behavior (avoidance of harm). Tusi's major work on ethics is his *Akhlaq-i-Nasiri* which not only contains his treatise on ethics, but on politics and economics, as well. Practical philosophy, for Tusi, was not complete without all three subjects being present.

Understanding: Understanding or deliberation is the highest level or perfection of consciousness of nature in its mode of operation.

Will of God: According to psychoethics, the Will of God flows through nature in its mode of operation, which is essentially the creative process.

BIBLIOGRAPHY

Arberry, A. J. (1950) *The Spiritual Physick of Rhazes*.. London:
    John Murray.
Avicenna. *Qanun* (1960). Translated by M. Thorenson. Lahore:
    Islamic Institute.
Browne, Edward G. (1921). *Arabian Medicine*. Lahore: Imprint.
Chishti, Hakim G. M. (1988). *The Traditional Healer's Hand-
    book*. Vermont: Healing Arts Press.
Chishti, Shaykh Hakim Moinuddin (1991). *The Book of Sufi
    Healing*. Vermont: Inner Traditions International, Ltd.
Chittick, William (1989). *The Sufi Path of Knowledge*. New
    York: State University Press.
Choudhery, G. W. (1991). *Islam and the Contemporary World*.
    Chicago: Kazi Publications, Inc.
Dawwani. (1876)*Akhlaq al-Jalali*. India Press: Lucknow.
(Algazel) Ghazali, Muhammad Ahmed (1962). *Ihya Ulum al-Din*.
    Translated by M. Fazul Karim.Dehli: Taj Company.
(Algazel) Ghazali, Muhammad Ahmed (1910). *al-Mizan al-Amal*.
    Cairo: Matba'at Kurdistan al-Ilmiyyah.
(Algazel) Ghazali, Muhammad Ahmed (1961). *Maqasid al-Fal-
    safiyh*. Cairo: Dar al-Ma'arif.
(Algazel) Ghazali, Muhammad Ahmed (1963). *Tahafut al-Fal-
    safah*. Translated by Sabih Ahmad Kamali. Pakistan:
    Pakistan Philosophical Congress.
Ehwany, Ahmed Fouad El- (1963). "Ibn Rushd (Averroes)." In
    M. M. Sharif (Ed.) *History of Muslim Philosophy*. Weis-
    baden: Otto Harrassowitz.
Haeri, Shaykh Fadhlalla (1989). *The Journey of the Self*. London:
    Element Books.
Hick, John (1989). *Three Faiths: One God*. NY: SUNY.
Ibn Ridwan, Ali (1984). Translated by Michael W. Dols. *Me-
    dieval Islamic Medicine*. Berkeley: University of Califor-
    nia Press.
McCarthy, R. J. (1980). *Freedom and Fulfillment: An Annotated*

Translation of al-Ghazali's al-Munqidh min al-Dalal and other Relevent Works of al-Ghazali. Boston: Twayne.

Ma'sumi, Muhammad Saghir Hasan al- (1963). "Ibn Bajjah (Avempace)." In M. M. Sharif, *History of Muslim Philosophy*. Weisbaden: Otto Harrassowitz.

Miskawayh, Ahmad ibn Muhammad (1968). *Tahdhib al-akhlaq*. Translated by Constantine K. Zurayk. Beirut: American University of Beirut.

Murata, Sachiko (1992). *The Tao of Islam*. New York: SUNY

Naraqi, Muhammad Mahdi ibn Abi Dharr (1987) *Jami al-Sa'adat*. Translated by Shahyar Sa'adat. Tehran: Foundation of Islamic Thought..

Nasr, Seyyid Hossein (1976). *Man and Nature*. London: Unwin Paperbacks.

Nasr, Seyyid Hossein (1981). *Islamic Life and Thought*. New York: SUNY Press.

Nurbakhsh, Javad (1954). *Dil va Nafs*. Tehran: Khaniqah Nimatullahi.

Peters, F. E. (1990). *Judaism, Christianity and Islam*. Princeton: Princeton University Press. 3 vols.

Rahman, Fazlur (1952). *Avicenna's Psychology*. Oxford: Oxford University Press.

Rahman, Fazlur (1989). *Health and Medicine in the IslamicTradition*. New York: Crossroad.

Razi, Fakhr al-Din (1960). *Ilm al-akhlaq*. Translated by M. Saghir Hasan Ma'sumi. New Delhi: Kitab Bhavan.

Riso, Don Richard (1992). *Discovering Your Personality Type*. Boston: Houghton Mifflin Company.

Rizvi, Syed Azhar Ali (1989). *Muslim Tradition in Psychotherapy and Modern Trends*. Lahore: Institute of Islamic Culture.

Rohr, Richard and Andreas Ebert (1990). *Discovering the Enneagram*. New York: Crossroad.

Sharif, M. M. (1962). *History of Muslim Philosophy*. Weisbaden: Otto Harrassowitz.

Sherif, Mohamed Ahmed (1975). *Ghazali's Theory of Virtue*.

New York: SUNY.

Siddiqui, Abdul Hameed (1991). *The Life of Muhammad*. Chicago: Kazi Publications, Inc.

Siddiqi, Bakhtyar Husain (1963). "Nasir al-Din Tusi." In M. M. Sharif, *History of Muslim Philosophy*. Weisbaden: Otto Harrassowitz.

Suhrawardi, Shihabuddin Yahya (1982). Translated by W. M. Thackston. *The Mystical and Visionary Treatises of Shihabuddin Yahya Suhrawardi*. London: The Octagon Press.

Tusi, Nasir al-Din 1964). *Akhlaq al-Nasiri*. Translated by G. Wickens. London: George Allen and Unwin.

Ulanov, Ann and Barry (1975). *Religion and the Unconscious*. Philadelphia: The Westminister Press.

General Index

Smelling 75
Social affairs 12
Social learning 127
Socratic method 84
Soul 7, 27, 29
Soul at peace 131
Source 29, 55, 91, 94
Spears 106
Species 55, 103, 113
Spheres, active 61
Spheres, passive 61
Spirit 4, 8, 10, 15, 29. 95
Spiritual truths 77
Straight Path 45, 69, 85
Structure 19
Struggle in the Way of God 11
Struggle, inward 11
Submission to the Will of God
    7, 8, 91
Substance, single 27
Sun 62
Sunnah 43
Sunshine 103
Surah Hud 45
Survival of the individual 93
Survival of the race 93
Swiftness in running 106

T
Ta'yid 5, 9, 10
Tabi'iya 81
Taharah 11
Takwini guidance 5, 6, 8, 9, 18,
    43, 44, 45, 51, 66, 70, 86, 90,
    117, 133, 134
Takwini guided 37
Takwini guided conscience 19
Tasdid 5, 9, 10
Tashri'i guidance 5, 7, 8, 9, 10,
    19, 43, 44, 45, 51, 66, 90, 102,
    117, 133, 134

Tashri'i guided 37
Taste 52, 55
Tasting 75
Tawhid 2
Temperament 39, 115
Temperance 12, 13, 32, 43, 44,
    45, 46, 86, 96, 114, 126, 134
Theology 32
Thought 65
Thought/action 76
Tongue 55
Topography 19
Touch 55
Touching 75
Tradition 12
Traditional method 13
Traditional personality para-
    digm 125, 126, 127, 128
Traditional perspective 1, 4, 6,
    29, 30, 38, 39, 51, 52, 84, 111
Traditional psychology 2, 4, 36
Trait (s) 39, 40
Traits, negative 133
Traits, positive 133
Transformation 38
Trees 103
Trickery 97
True perfection 116
Trust 5, 10, 15, 18, 19, 134
Trust of nature 7, 27
Trustee 5, 15, 18, 19
Trusteeship 11, 15, 18
Truth 134
Tusi 74
Tyranny 72
Tyranny of the self 91

U
Unconscious aspects of self
    133
Unconscious function 32, 45,